HOW TO USE YOUR CREDIT RATING TO PUT YOU ON THE PATH TO DEBT FREEDOM

A GUIDE TO HELP THE AVERAGE PERSON BREAKTHROUGH DEBT AND POVERTY BY BECOMING YOUR OWN BANK AND HARD MONEY LENDER

G.E.S. BOLEY JR., MBA

CONTENTS

INTRODUCTION

"If you realize the value of controlling a large amount of wealth and consider how you can prepare yourself to gather such an amount, then the concept of becoming your own bank will appeal to you."

Someone once said that if all the money in the world were equally distributed among all people, in ten years or so, most of the money would be controlled by the select few. There is no way we can validate this statement, but if you think about it, it's not far away from the truth. But ask yourself, why would this happen? The answer is quite simple, really. Most people don't know the first thing about banking and how it affects their lives.

Among all the businesses in the world, banking is the most vital one. Without banking, all other businesses will cease. In every transaction, money flows from one end to another within a short period of time, otherwise there is no business. There must be a supply source present for the money to flow. Therein lies the essence of the banking business. An organization or an individual controls a large pool of money that must flow to fulfill a purpose.

There is a single reservoir of money in our world. Various countries with their own currencies, along with corporations, companies, and banks manage this reservoir. It can be compared to the Earth's Ocean system. Three-quarters of the Earth's surface is water. Due to the heat of the sun, some of the water evaporates and enters the atmosphere which leads to wind currents. These currents carry the water vapor across the earth where it falls to the ground in the form of snow, sleet, and rain.

Some of this water flows through all of us; we cannot survive without it. This is what makes it so important. And where does all the water end up? In the oceans of course! This is the perfect metaphor for the banking business. We draw some money from the reservoir to use as we please, but in the end, it returns to the banking system.

It all comes down to how much control you have over the banking function as it serves your purposes. This book is about creating a banking system of your own so you have total control over your needs and become your own bank. By paying careful attention, you make drastic positive changes to your financial condition.

The concept of Infinite banking is not a new one. For centuries, people have been drawing money out of their life insurance policies. Just imagine you have a bank of your own, containing your own money, that you can take loans from whenever needed. Every time you take a loan, you pay the interest and the principal to yourself. So, you are making money from the interest instead of the bank.

Instead of relying on a traditional institution to lend you money, you can finance yourself and be your own bank. It may sound like an impossible task at first, but several people are already financing themselves and getting good results. When most people take a look at their finances, all they see are the immediate issues. Very few are able to think long-term, and they realize how important life insurance is. They realize that the actions they take today will affect them and their families in the future.

You must be thinking, what is the purpose of being your own bank? What problems does it solve? Let us start with the basics. To gain wealth in terms of services and goods, you have to use a monetary value known as capital. There are two ways you can do this. You can sell the asset in which capital is built, or you can leverage the asset, i.e. think of it as collateral and borrow money from a third party.

Most people prefer to use capital through leverage, and it is quite effective if done the right way. However, a continued dependency is something you should avoid fostering through your leveraging. Leverage is more efficient than liquidation or selling, and so it is preferred by most. This way, you can utilize the services of assets you are acquiring and that which you are collateralizing, simultaneously.

While surveying your assets to determine which are suitable to build capital in, you may want to review the leveraging terms. You should consider how they might benefit you and how much control you would retain over your asset after you leverage it in this manner. Questions you should ask: Are there any restrictions on what way you can use the borrowed money? What roadblocks must be cleared for successful leveraging?

When it comes to credit transactions, these are difficult and costly obstacles. In the worst-case scenario, the lender is concerned about not getting their money back, even when they have the option of seizing the collateral agreed upon. This is due to the fact that collateral's future value cannot always be determined. The value of the property depends on what people are willing to pay for it, and we can never tell today what the value of a particular property will be in the future.

The price inflation of constant assets has been the subject of unrealistic projections by financial advisors and monetary authorities. But this changes when you use well-structured insurance that pays dividends. By becoming your own bank, you can eliminate the uncertainties. With other assets, guaranteeing the future value is not possible, but with life insurance, the lender can do this easily.

You must be wondering why. This whole asset is a series of promises which are contract bound. The prices of housing and such are bound to fluctuate, and the person lending the mortgage is not able to control it, but the cash value of your life will continue to increase as you keep paying the premiums. But how is this possible? How can an organization state with surety that the value of an asset will keep rising? The answer to this question lies in the computational relationship between cash value, death benefit, and premium.

This cash value can be mathematically represented as the difference between the premium that is due and the death benefit. As you pay premium after premium, the amount that gets subtracted from the death benefit starts to get smaller and smaller, thus increasing the difference. So provided you keep paying the premium, the cash value is guaranteed to rise. Since an irrefutable mathematical law dictates this relationship, the insurance company has no qualms about backing the contract.

Another self-funding option you can consider is business credit funding. This is a great alternative to a startup loan and this can help you get started by establishing a business credit line and separating personal and business finances. In order to qualify for a business credit card, you need to have a certain combined income and a good personal credit score, which the lenders will consider. Business credit cards might ask you to give a personal guarantee but never collateral. You will also get sign-up bonuses and be able to access the rewards program.

Many small businesses these days, including my businesses, use business credit cards for funding their operations. It is advisable that you choose a card with 0% interest rate. This way, you can make purchases and maintain a balance for up to 15 months without any interest while still running your business.

Sometimes it might be difficult to secure a business credit, in which case, personal funding is another option to consider. It is a great way to start off a business, although it might be risky if you don't monitor all your expenses. After using your personal funds to launch a business, you can establish business credit which will give you access to more capital in the years to come. A personal credit card can allow you to make the initial purchases required to start off your business.

You need to carefully monitor credit utilization and always remember to make your bill payments because business expenses can be quite high and it might destroy your credit history if you're not careful. If you're feeling brave, you can take out money from your savings account, and if you have a substantial amount set aside, it can be a cheap way to jump-start your business. You can also take home equity loans or take a portion of your retirement savings and invest it in your company.

This book will teach you how to have better control over your money. This means no more multiple visits to the bank, filling out an endless number of applications, and waiting for long hours to see whether you qualify for a decent interest rate or not. It also means you don't have to pay any more fees for origination and application. This way, you can do whatever you want with your money. By cutting banks out of the equation, you can retain more money and continue to build your wealth with impunity.

You will also learn how to limit the transfer of your wealth. Of course, it is not possible to stop it all at once, but you can stop it from being transferred to financial companies, credit unions, the government, and Wall Street. You will have full control over your wealth and who it gets transferred to. This can be friends, family, or some cause you care about. Becoming your own banker is beneficial because you can determine who profits from your wealth and financial decisions, and you get to decide when and how this wealth is transferred to those parties.

In this book, you will get to know how to imitate a bank by recycling, reusing, and recapturing your money, which is an excellent way to accumulate wealth. The multiplier effect comes into play when it comes to recycling, reusing, and recapturing your money. By getting easy access to money, you can keep reusing it, investing it, and keeping it moving. Helping you to build wealth faster on your terms.

Normally, you will be able to access 90% of your wealth whenever you want. And what's more, you don't even need to pay any fees or penalties for this. You will also be able to access your money quicker, within 1 to 20 business days depending on what self-funding instrument you have. This wouldn't be possible if you keep your money in a traditional bank.

By learning about the whole life insurance policy, you will learn how to build equity. It is similar to a home policy where you can extract loans against equity, and the fundamental policy continues to expand. By using equity as collateral, you activate the multiplier effect and are able to accumulate more wealth in a short span of time.

Also, by learning how to be your own banker, you can access your money in multiple ways. You can take a loan, leveraged dividends, and withdraw an amount from the cash value. Even when you take a loan, you will get to decide when and how to repay it. So long as you keep funding the policy, you can do anything you want with your wealth.

If you need more proof that the concept of being your own bank as mentioned in this book will help you out, you need to consider that the best -rated life insurance companies provide you with a strong foundation upon which you can build your wealth. Many of these companies have been around for more than a century. On the other hand, many of the banks are not as stable as they claim to be, as they often have vast leverage amounts. Moreover, the derivatives market sees some activity from these banks which is a bit concerning.

It is estimated that by the end of 2017, the number of derivatives in the marketplace will be $157 trillion. So your life insurance acts as a safe bucket rather than an investment, providing a strong foundation from where you can carry out your personal financing, free from the influence of the big banks and Wall Street.

Furthermore, the infinite banking policy is focused on cash accumulation and not on the death benefit. So you will learn how to overfund the policy by putting the maximum amount of money into it while remaining within the bounds of an insurance policy. You will be able to use your money for making other purchases, which will increase the speed of your money. By keeping your cash value as collateral, you can take a life insurance loan against it.

Perhaps the biggest proof of this book benefiting you is that your policy loans and cash value will not be reflected in our credit report when you practice infinite banking. So even if you have a large outstanding loan, you will still be able to take out other loans. Moreover, there are no qualifications required for life insurance roles, and you can borrow or withdraw whenever you want.

I can promise that with this book, you can enjoy the mental peace that comes with steady annual growth. This is backed up by the fact that in its 150-year history, the infinite banking strategy hasn't had a bad year. It has survived the Great Depression and the Great Recession, so you can safely bank on it. With these traditional retirement policies, you never really know how much retirement savings are guaranteed, but with infinite banking, you'll always be aware of this value.

I can also promise that you will learn how to bypass banks and credit card companies by financing your business, college education, vacations, and cars by yourself. You will be able to get whatever amount of money you need. Many famous personalities like J.C. Penney, Ray Kroc, and Walt Disney used this technique to expand their businesses when they were refused loans from several banks.

After going through this book, you will know how to access the wealth in your plan without any restrictions or penalties imposed by the government. Moreover, the money extracted from the policy will continue to expand, even after you've used it for investments and purchases. And then there is the promise of tax advantages, which alone should make you learn about being your own bank. By taking advantage of tax-free withdrawals and delayed tax growth, you can protect yourself from higher tax amounts during your retirement.

Finally, I can promise that learning how to become your own bank will allow you to better protect your assets, so you don't need to worry about losing assets in a legal dispute or in business. The market is quite unpredictable, but with a whole life insurance policy, the value of your assets will grow continuously at the same rate mentioned in the contract.

If you ask a financier for advice, they will most likely tell you that you should invest your money. But doesn't it seem strange that no one would advise you regarding how to maximize your control over your money? Money is considered necessary for an individual to make real changes in their life, and to exercise their will in the real world. Then where are all the grand strategies about acquiring money and how to use, grow, and protect it?

Investing is the exact opposite of gathering wealth for the purpose of using it. As many have argued, the idea of investing is mostly about giving up the control you have over your money. The rest of it is the objective to generate a financial gain. But this gain is not possible without control. In investments, you relinquish control over your money to the person controlling the investments so they can make your money work and give you the return from it.

A subject that is not explored much is how to accumulate financial value and control it. This financial value doesn't only refer to wealth or the amount of money in your savings account. It refers to capital, which is the property's financial value and which you can use to buy other properties. For example, if you have a certain amount of money inside your safe that you want to use to buy a car, that is capital for you. It is the monetary value of the cash property that you want to spend to buy a car (another property).

In modern finance, capital is often neglected. Every once in a while, someone does something groundbreaking with their capital and everyone sings praises about them, but as always, after the excitement has died down, everyone forgets about capital. Capital is not what gets you involved. Like most of us, you started a business to make a living and gain profits. You bought a house so that you could live in it. You bought bitcoin, silver, and gold so that you could sell them at high prices at a later point in time. Get my point?

Capital is considered as a side-benefit, and when something goes wrong, it becomes a side-problem when there is a lack of it. If the housing market is unfavorable, you might consider selling your house. The value a banker places on your business is never quite the same as what you consider it to be. The prices of bitcoin, silver, and gold can fall at any time, making your capital negative. So the current value of the asset is now less than what you paid to acquire it, and this can be really frustrating.

If there are severe problems with the neglected capital, the situation may be more than frustrating. You may have to close down the shop and the bank might seize your assets. This is the result of you treating capital like a side-problem rather than treating it as a source of financial prosperity and opportunity. That is where the concept of being your own bank comes to the rescue.

This concept, discussed in detail in the book, teaches you the best way to build and utilize capital. It allows you to exert control over massive amounts of wealth. And it is true that the ones who control capital will control those who fail to deploy and build some capital of their own.

If you realize the value of controlling a large amount of wealth and consider how you can prepare yourself to gather such an amount, then the concept of becoming your own bank will appeal to you. The truth is, we cannot discuss investment without discussing capital first, because investing for those holding a large amount of capital is drastically different from investing for the people who do not have much capital.

So if you want to have greater control over your capital, then you must read this book, as it will teach you how you can benefit by paying attention to capital through a whole life insurance policy and other capital sources. As mentioned, in those policies, the lender of the loan guarantees the collateral value which is a unique phenomenon in the world of finance. Rather than running your money through various banks, you can create your own money ecosystem which results in compound interest growth. So even if you are borrowing against the cash value, the money in your policy continues to be at work.

Reference Links

https://medium.com/@ryandgriggs/why-should-i-build-capital-with-the-infinite-banking-concept-ffd5fdcb9fd8

https://truthspress.files.wordpress.com/2012/10/770-accounts-becoming-your-own-banker-unlock-the-infinite-banking-conceptf-pdf.pdf

https://corporatefinanceinstitute.com/resources/knowledge/finance/infinite-banking/

https://thecollegeinvestor.com/21605/understanding-infinite-banking/

https://fee.org/articles/an-introduction-to-the-infinite-banking-concept/

https://www.eaglebusinesscredit.com/blog/business-credit-and-how-to-get-funding/

CHAPTER ONE: UNDERSTANDING FINANCING AND QUICK FIX LOANS

"Payday loans could also impact your chances of taking a future loan or a mortgage. Even if you are able to pay back your loan in its entirety and before the due date, the very fact that you took a loan will cause lenders to shun you because they will realize that you were going through financial troubles."

ONE DAY, YOU MIGHT FIND THAT YOU DO NOT HAVE enough funds in your bank account to pay a bill. Many people who seem to find themselves in this situation, opt for a payday loan. They have gained a fair amount of popularity as they offer a quick way of acquiring some money and adding it to your bank account when the need is urgent. In the USA, approximately 12 million people take payday loans every year. But have you ever considered how dangerous an impact such loans could have on your wallet?

Payday loans and auto loans are both subjects of heavy marketing and advertising. They offer quick approval or fast cash, but at the same time, they come at a heavy price. Compared to other financial products, these loans are pretty expensive, and the interest rates are 10-20 times higher than that of a credit card. So instead of lifting families out of poverty, they act as a leaky boat that slowly drowns individuals and families in debt and leads them along the path of financial ruin.

Payday loans are high-cost, short-term loans amounting to $500 or less. These loans are usually paid back by the borrower on the next paycheck day. Payday loans can be of various types, like cash advance loans, deferred deposit loans, post-dated check loans, and check advance loans. Before applying for a payday loan online or visiting the store of a payday lender, you need to go through a series of steps.

These include providing your personal and financial information, telling the lender how much money you need to borrow, securing your loan by check or debit information from your bank account, paying a borrower's fee, and finally, having the cash ready before leaving the office of the lender and depositing it directly into your account. But before taking yourself through these steps, you should know what you're getting into.

For both payday loans and auto loans, the annual interest is more than 300 percent, and there are high chances you will have to take another loan to pay off the first one. In the United States, these loans take approximately $8 billion in fees and interest from struggling communities and families while putting a huge sum of money in the lenders' wallet.

You need to pay a fee to take out a payday loan and this might lie anywhere between 10-30 dollars per 100 dollars borrowed. Depending on the amount of money you are borrowing, this can be a considerable sum of money. For example, if you take a loan with a fee of $15 per $100 for two weeks, that means you get a 400% APR.

Moreover, you can land yourself in a lot of financial trouble if you cannot pay back your payday loans. The longer the duration of the loan, the more fees you have to pay to the lender. If a long time has passed and you still cannot pay back your payday loan, it will lead to larger problems that you'd want to avoid.

Payday loans could also impact your chances of taking a future loan or a mortgage. Even if you are able to pay back your loan in its entirety and before the due date, the very fact that you took a loan will cause lenders to shun you because they will realize that you were going through financial troubles. If you took more than one payday loan within a few months, it acts as a huge red flag for lenders. Lenders are reluctant to lend money to individuals with a history of payday loans, even if they have all been paid for. Some of them even state explicitly that they won't lend money to individuals having payday loans on their credit.

The cost of payday loans is excessive and unnecessary. Although they might not be available readily, there are better credit options borrowers can choose from. There are also noncredit options available, which do not cause the same degree of financial loss and pose fewer risks. These options include public assistance programs, religious congregations, and seeking help from friends and family.

In the USA, payday loans are banned in 14 states, and in the District of Columbia, due to a cap being placed on state interest rates. But in some communities, like in Texas, these lenders are seemingly omnipotent and they prey on vulnerable communities, outnumbering even grocery stores. Often, they are to whom desperate people turn in times of dire need.

Auto title lending andpayday lean entered the scene in the 1990s, and they exist even today due to heavy lobbying and abysmal economic conditions. The Federal Reserve states that approximately 50% of Americans would not be able to procure $400 without selling an asset or borrowing money from someone. Furthermore, the minimum wage hasn't been raised by the policymakers to help people deal with the inflation that is there for decades now.

As a direct result of this, The minimum wage today is $7.25 per hour which is much lower than the minimum wage in 1968, adjusted due to inflation, which in today's money would amount to $10 per hour. There is a lack of assistance for disadvantaged and vulnerable families, and this coupled with insufficient wages increases the chances of families opting for expensive credit to remain financially stable.

In the year 2017, the US government agency known as the Consumer Financial Protection Bureau (CFPB) set a rule to control these expensive loans. But now, the CFPB wants to revise the rule and get rid of the provision regarding the ability of the borrower to pay the money back. The essence of this rule is that a lender should check if a borrower would be able to pay the money back before lending them money. Getting rid of this provision will enable the payday loan companies to use their loans with high-interest rates against customers who are exceptionally vulnerable.

So it is clear that consumer protections must be enacted and defended, along with setting state laws like interest rate caps. Apart from taking steps to address financial aggression, policymakers should look to create inclusive economies and protect economically disadvantaged communities to take care of the financial instability that draws these families to these troublesome financial products.

Several families across the country take out auto title loans and payday loans and later they struggle to manage their finances. More often than not, these loans are not used for specific emergencies, but for recurring financial troubles. It has been seen that people of color and women tend to take out more payday loans. In fact, 52% of people who borrow payday loans are female, while African Americans are 2 times as likely to take a loan, compared to others. This shows the stark wage and wealth gaps between demographics, as well as the innumerable payday loan centers cropping up in Latino and African American neighborhoods.

In the year 2006, a Christian ministry in Charlottesville known as Love Inc conducted a survey on people who reached out to them seeking financial assistance. About 60% of them were knee-deep in debt and required to pay back their payday loans. Other ministries and churches across America report similar trends. The payday lenders target people in the low-income bracket, who are too desperate and stressed out to realize that they are headed for a debt trap.

You will find payday lenders arguing that it is mandatory for borrowers to read the terms and conditions and think about the financial implications of taking a loan. But during times of desperation, individuals are in no state of mind to grasp the future implications of their present actions. Churches across the country are realizing the adverse effects of payday loans and how they are indirectly causing poverty in the community. People who take out payday loans are more likely to be neglectful about their credit cards and become bankrupt than people in a similar financial situation who don't opt for such loans. Due to excessive bank account deficits, families taking payday loans are likely to be late in paying their bills, delaying the purchase of prescription drugs and medical care.

As we know, since the 1970s, wages in the USA have remained more or less stagnant, in spite of the enhancement in worker productivity. Middle-class wages saw a brief rise in the 1990s, but apart from that, they have been pretty much stagnant since the 70s. This is putting middle-class families at risk and they are edging closer to the poverty line. So much so that about 50% of Americans are expected to spend at least a year being poor or near-poor.

The federal minimum wage has remained the same for

the last six years, and in fact, it has lost its value by almost a quarter since 1968, when it was adjusted due to the inflation. On top of that, the economy is growing and is quite demanding, which has led to unpredictable income and volatile work schedules for workers who earn low wages, which is a group consisting largely of women and people of color. So if the business is not doing good, even if the employee is not at fault, they might run into financial trouble and not be able to meet their basic expenses.

This wealth stagnation has been going on for decades now and this is compounded by the wealth gap that keeps families from saving money for the future and meeting their immediate needs. An alarming statistic reveals that between the years 1983 and 2013, the average total value of families belonging to the lower-income strata of society decreased by 18% while the average net worth of high-income families almost doubled. We should also consider the racial wealth gap, whereas, in 2013, the average net worth of Latino households was $13,700, while that of African American households was $11,000. This is extremely low compared to the average net worth of Caucasian households, which was $141,900.

There have been some recent changes in public assistance programs that have further widened the wage gap, especially during emergency situations. In 1996, Congress passed the Personal Responsibility and Work Opportunity Reconciliation Act, which was a hard blow to welfare. Earlier, there used to be a program that would give financial assistance to low-income individuals, but this was replaced by the TANF (Temporary Assistance for Needy Families) program which had strict eligibility criteria and also placed time limits on the receipt.

This, in the long-term, has reduced the amount of cash assistance provided to disadvantaged families. Also since

1996, the TANF block grant has lost 30% of its value, and incentives are provided to the state for diverting funds from financial assistance. As a result, out of 4 TANF dollars, only 1 is used for aiding needy families. Towards the beginning, TANF helped 68% of families, but now the percentage has been significantly reduced to 23%.

TANF is not the only public assistance program that has witnessed a steady decline. The one-time short-term benefits of TANF that offered temporary aid to needy families during emergencies are not as beneficial as they were twenty years ago when the program was called Emergency Assistance. Back then, it wasn't block-granted and provided effective aid to families.

But then, nonrecurrent benefits expenditures got adjusted due to the inflation and declined greatly. In 2015, the total state and federal funds dedicated to this aid were $865 million, compared to $1.4 billion in 1995 for federal funds only. Meanwhile, funding for the CSBG (Community Services Block Grant) program where local agencies help out low-income families by funding emergency services, nutrition, and employment, has also declined since its inception in 1982. Taking population growth and inflation into account, funding for the CSBG has declined by 35% since 1982 and 15% since 2000.

With the recent changes in the labor market and the economy, the unemployment insurance (UI) program which was created to help families remain financially stable during unemployment has become less effective. Only 25% of unemployed workers received UI benefits in 2015. The figure is lower (20%) in 13 states. This combined effect of declining public assistance programs, inflation, and wage inequality has made disadvantaged families more vulnerable to lenders who exploit them for their own gains.

Today, the government relies heavily on tax expenditures

for addressing poverty, and this is a big challenge for financial security. The Child Tax Credit and the EITC (Educational Improvement Tax Credit) are considered to be some of the best policies for alleviating poverty. In 2014, 9.8 million Americans were able to come out of poverty due to these programs. But these tax credits come in lump-sum amounts and most families usually save them for the future or use them for making big purchases.

Consequently, most of these families suffer from financial insecurity for the remaining part of the year. A number of EITC recipients were interviewed in 2007 and they responded that almost 25% of the money they received from EITC was spent for repaying debts. Financial products such as refund anticipation loans have been the subject of regulatory crackdowns, but still many individuals tend to borrow money against tax refunds. Since the tax credits are in lump-sum form, many families resort to unscrupulous loans in the meantime.

Since 2009, the FDIC (Federal Deposit Insurance Corporation) conducts surveys twice every year. In 2017, this survey collected data from over 35,000 families to determine the percentage of US households not having an insured institution account and the percentage that possess bank accounts but have procured the services of alternative financial institutions in the past year. The insights provided by this survey also aid efforts to better serve the needs of banking system consumers.

According to the 2017 survey estimates, 6.5% of families in the US were not associated with any bank. This includes about 8.4 million families. Additionally, 18.7% of families in the US representing 24.2 million households were under-banked, indicating that in spite of having savings and checking accounts with banks, they sought out the help of financial services and products that lay outside the banking system.

The payday lenders profited not only from the fluctuating economic climate, but also changes in the way credentials are used. Due to a Supreme Court ruling in 1978, the state's power to limit interest rates got limited. Furthermore, they introduced legislation emphasizing the national bank's ability to dictate insurance rates. Due to the growth of the industry during the 90s, payday lenders started encouraging legislation enabling and exploiting loopholes, thus allowing them to bypass the rate caps.

Auto title loans and payday loans often spell doom for families. Rather than solving the financial issues of families, they add to their distress, due to which they face the risk of foreclosure and eviction. Many borrowers struggle to care for their children and to maintain the stability of their family, and some even lose their jobs due to repossessed cars.

An overwhelming 80% of auto title and payday loans lead to other loans since the borrowers cannot afford to pay for essential expenses. The average borrower of payday loans remains in debt for six months or so. In fact, 15% of new payday loans result in 10 subsequent loans. On average, payday loan borrowers take 8 loans in one year, resulting in an interest of $520 on a loan amount of $375, which can be higher in some cases.

Auto title and payday loan lenders have access to a customer's card or bank account, which means they become a priority expense. Borrowers who are already financially weak, then struggle to manage their personal finances and prioritize essentials such as rent, medicines, hygiene, etc. About 25% of loan borrowers cannot make their payments on time, due to which their bank accounts are closed, making managing money a tough task.

About 20% of borrowers get their vehicles repossessed or

seized when they are unable to make payments, and even after this, the entire debt might not be paid. The traditional credit of the borrower gets affected and credit card owners are very likely to neglect their credit cards upon taking out a payday loan.

This leads to a ripple effect that influences the family budgets. A study conducted in 2011 revealed that families belonging to the lower-income strata residing near a state where it is legal for payday lenders to lend money are very likely to face trouble paying their rent and mortgage. This eventually leads to foreclosure or eviction, which is hard not only for the families but also for the communities they live in.

Housing instability eventually leads to homelessness which hampers the mental and physical health of families and also affects the children's education. This also leads to families moving into dubious housing arrangements where there are safety hazards and the neighborhoods are unsafe. Housing instability is a curse that leaves borrowers without a steady income and may also lead to loss of jobs.

So taxpayers pay the price, no matter what. They have to bear the cost of incarceration, medical treatment, and emergency shelter. Taking out payday loans leaves families without many funds and as a result, they have to rely on public assistance. In areas where payday loans are legal and accessible, people tend to enroll themselves more in the Supplemental Nutrition Assistance Program (SNAP).

The implications of predatory payday loans extend well beyond homelessness and repossession of cars. The debt can lead to domestic tension and family instability. Payday loan borrowers are often unable to pay for child support, as all their money is spent on essentials and paying back their loans. Consequently, the recipients of child support lose a vital source of money, and parents not having custody of their children get their wages and assets seized, their licenses suspended and even imprisoned. Not only does this complicate the debt repayment, but it also intensifies the conflict between the two parties.

Reference Links

https://www.responsiblelending.org/sites/default/files/uploads/modern-day-usury-the-payday-loan-trap.pdf
http://stopthedebttrap.org/about/whatispaydaylending/
https://money.howstuffworks.com/personal-finance/banking/payday-loans2.htm
https://www.1stsource.com/advice/personal/credit-and-debt/credit/article/watch-out-for-payday-loans
https://www.lsfcu.org/how-to-steer-clear-of-payday-lending-traps/

CHAPTER TWO: HOW YOUR CREDIT HELPS AND HURTS YOU

"Your credit rating not only affects the approval of your loan but also determines the rate of interest at which you will need to repay the loan."

A LOAN IS ESSENTIALLY A CONTRACTUAL PROMISE, AND the credit rating tells the lender how likely you are to pay back the loan amount while adhering to the agreement. When the credit rating is high, it means you will most likely pay back the entire loan without any problems. A low credit rating tells a lender that the individual has a history of not being able to pay back their loans and they might continue this pattern of behavior in their future dealings.

Your score determines whether you'll get approved or not for a loan or whether you will receive favorable terms for the same. While credit scores apply to individuals only, credit ratings are applicable for government bodies and businesses. Agencies like TransUnion, Experian, and Equifax maintain a credit-card history and your lender can find your credit score from any one of them. Usually, your credit score will be represented as a number lying between 300 and 850.

In earlier days, long-term credit ratings were given more importance, which predicted the likelihood of the borrower defaulting at any time in the future. But these days there is more emphasis on short-term rating, which tells the lender the likelihood of you defaulting within the time span of a year.

In the USA, people use credit in every aspect of life, both for business and personal dealings. If you have a decent credit rating, you can get approved for small business loans and credit cards, automobile loans, get better insurance rates, rent an apartment or a home, and be qualified for a home mortgage. Sometimes people immigrating to the United States are not aware of the fact that credit history is a non-transferable entity and your credit score in your home country means nothing here. So they need to build their credit so they can take loans, use credit cards, and engage in other business-related activities that demand a good credit score.

While the borrower will always try to maintain a high credit rating to get themselves a favorable interest rate, the credit rating agency must assess your financial situation objectively to determine your capacity of repaying the debt. Your credit rating not only affects the approval of your loan but also determines the rate of interest at which you will need to repay the loan. For many companies, getting a loan is vital for paying their expenses, and things can turn disastrous if the loan is denied or if the interest rate is too high.

Your credit rating tells you which lenders are likely to offer you a loan. For a guy with a perfect credit score, getting a loan is a piece of cake, but if yours is poor or just decent, your options are indeed limited. For an investor, on the other hand, the credit rating of a company determines how safe it is to purchase their bonds. It is risky to invest in a company with a poor credit rating, as it indicates that they might not be able to make their bond payments.

It is vital for a borrower to always keep an eye on his credit rating and work towards improving their score. Credit ratings are dynamic values, and they can change in the blink of an eye. A single negative debt can ruin a perfect credit score. Generally, debtors prefer entities with good credit scores and long credit histories. This is because having a short credit history tells them nothing about whether you can maintain a good credit score consistently over the years.

I find it surprising that not a single high school all over the country teaches its students about credit scores. This is something that everyone should know in order not to make bad decisions that lower their credit scores and prevent them from taking loans and mortgages. I had to save money for five years after marriage until I had enough for making my down payment on a mortgage. But because I had made the minimum payment on my credit card debt, some banks saw red. I always made my payments on time and I never thought I would have any problems with a mortgage.

Although I was able to get the mortgage eventually, it was at a much higher rate. I had to work with this high-interest rate for 12 months until I was able to get a lower rate for myself by refinancing my loan. Because I was clueless about my credit report and I didn't know that the details of my credit card usage and how I managed the balance would affect my interest rate. If I had more prior knowledge regarding credit rating, I would have saved myself a large amount of money.

Your credit card usage percentage affects your credit score and lenders, creditors, and underwriters carefully consider these factors. The credit utilization ratio is an important parameter used to determine how much you are using your credit card. It is calculated by dividing the amount of credit you are using currently by the amount that is available. For instance, if you have a $5,000 balance in one credit card, and the total available credit is $10,000, then you have a 50% credit utilization rate.

A low credit utilization rate tells the lenders that you are not using too much of the available credit. This gives you a good credit score and it indicates that you do not overspend and are good at managing credit. So in order to attain a good credit score, you should keep your spending to a minimum. Having a higher credit score lets you secure credit cards, mortgages, and auto loans with considerable ease. In order to get favorable interest rates, your personal credit card usage should be under 20%, and your business credit card should be under 50%.

On January 23, 2020, a new FICO credit scoring model was announced. Credit reporting agencies like Equifax, TransUnion, and Experian will be using these brand new scoring models for assessing the credit history of borrowers from the end of this year. Debts and late payments shall receive much more severe treatment in the new model, but your credit card history related to payment amounts and balances will also be considered. This is likely to change your existing FICO score.

Fair Isaac Corp, also known as FICO, last changed its credit score model back in 2014 through the release of FICO Score 9. The model is called FICO Score 10 Suite, and it includes FICO 10 T Score and FICO 10 Score. This new credit scoring model version will process information as before, but there are several crucial differences that you should know about.

The previous FICO models used five principal factors to assess your credit score, which included new credit accounts, credit mix, credit history age, owed amounts, and payment history. These factors are expected to remain unchanged in the new model. What the new FICO 10 model aims to do is to provide lenders with a more accurate understanding of the credit risk you possess. FICO 10 brings something new to the table by doing something that previous models did not do: It takes into account the trended data.

Trended data is also known as time-series data, and it displays information on the credit report revealing how you have dealt with our accounts over the last 2 years, thus creating a clear picture of your financial condition. So, if you have made late payments in the past, it is likely to affect your credit score. This is a shift from the previous credit scoring models where the impact of late payments was not as serious.

Your credit report consists of data related to your credit card accounts, and the trended data reflects 2 years worth of data including the minimum amount to be paid, on your balances, and the amount of money you paid according to your latest statements. This way, the FICO 10 can distinguish customers paying their entire outstanding debt amounts every month from those individuals who carry forward their balance from one month to another. The former group is known as transactors, and since they pay their credit card bills in full every month, they are assigned higher credit scores and are considered to be less of a credit risk than those who keep revolving their balance.

With the help of trended data, the FICO 10 model can determine the fluctuations in your balance over a certain period of time. As in, it reveals whether you are increasing, maintaining, or reducing your balance. By considering these factors, the new scoring model can predict credit risk, thus enabling both the lenders and the consumers to make more prudent decisions in regards to credit.

Rather than investing in a single score, FICO put in efforts to develop both FICO 10 T and FICO 10 so lenders can be more flexible in their approach and select the one which is most suitable. This has serious implications on the borrower, who now has to pay their bills on time or better, pay in advance to clear their credit card debt, before applying for any form of credit in the future.

Your new credit report will contain trended payment reports and you will be rewarded by VantageScore 4.0 and FICO 10 T if you have taken efforts to reduce your credit card balance. This way you can get favorable interest rates and save some money along the way.

When you've not made a payment on your credit debt, delinquency is said to have occurred. If after the due date, 30 days have passed, and you've still not made the payment, the lender will report you to the credit bureau. These late payment records adversely affect your credit score, as it questions your ability to pay your dues on time. No matter what the scoring model is, or how the credit score is generated, a late payment leads to a bad credit score that will remain in your record for several years.

The ramifications of late payments are more prominent with the new FICO Score 10 Suite than with the previous models. You will experience a bigger drop in your credit score if you fail to make your payments that you would under the former credit scoring models from FICO.

In order to avoid the consequences of late payments, it is advisable that you complete all of your payments within the stipulated time without any exceptions. For this, you can set up an autopay feature so that even if just a little amount is to be paid before the due date, you don't miss it. You can make larger chunks of payment in the middle of the month to ease your burden. This will allow your credit score to be decent. So no matter what the current scoring model is, always paying your dues on time is a foolproof way of maintaining good credit scores.

As discussed earlier, your credit utilization rate has a great impact on your credit score, and while this has always been the case, with FICO 10, the impact will be more prominent.

There are many ways you can lower your credit utilization. First of all, you can avoid huge balances and use your credit card as little as possible to lower the rate.

If the bank issuing the credit card decides to increase the credit limit for you, the utilization percentage will improve, as in it will decrease, until and unless you use more than the credit limit. Also, if you have credit cards that you rarely use or don't use at all, you should keep them open, as this will mean you're not using the credit limit. This counts towards credit history and lower utilization and will improve your credit score.

FICO 10 will also treat personal loans differently than the previous FICO versions, and if your credit report has any personal loans, it will lower your credit score. This is a noticeable shift from how personal loan accounts have always been treated by FICO Scores. Personal loans, also known as signature loans, are installment loans that people usually use to pay off their credit card debts. This is known as debt consolidation, where a lower interest personal loan is taken out to pay off a credit card debt having a higher rate of interest.

For many years, people have been using the debt consolidation strategy to improve the credit score. It has long been considered as an excellent financial move since the interest rates for personal loans are much lower than the credit card rates. This way, you can make an installment loan out of your outstanding credit card debt, thus improving your credit score. If you have a lot of credit card debt and wish to eliminate it, this is a pretty effective strategy, even under the new credit scoring model.

Personal loans are unsecured while some lenders require a personal guarantee, have long been associated with high credit risk, but there are certain situations where your FICO 10 T and FICO 10 scores can improve due to an unsecured personal loan. An exemption to this rule is also there and we must take a look at this. If you pay off your credit card debts using a personal loan and then use the same cards to purchase new stuff, your balance will increase while you're paying off the loan. In this situation, your FICO 10 score will get damaged. So you should avoid a scenario wherein the process of paying off your credit card debts with unsecured loans, you incur additional credit card debts.

Those who already have a good FICO score do not need to worry, as, under FICO 10, their scores will most likely improve. But if you have a low FICO score, it will likely decrease further under FICO 10. Customers with low credit scores will have lower scores under the new credit scoring model. The credit reporting agencies will determine if your credit score qualifies for a FICO score, and if it doesn't, it certainly won't qualify for a FICO 10 score. There are a number of data standards that your credit report must satisfy. Only then can it be scored under one of the FICO credit scoring models.

The credit reporting agency Experian will be launching a new credit score product suite known as Experian Lift which will combine trended data, alternative credit, and traditional credit to put together a clearer picture of the creditworthiness of a consumer. This will allow them to prepare a credit score for a consumer who lacks a traditional credit file. This way, more consumers will be able to access credit products. The score range will remain the same for FICO 10. As in the previous version, the score will range from 300 to 850.

So, if you manage to slightly adjust the traditional way of managing your credit, you can earn a pretty high credit score under the new model. The basic techniques of maintaining low balances, sparingly applying for credit, and paying bills on time are still as effective as before. But since FICO 10 will consider trended data as well, it is important that you avoid carrying high balances on credit cards for too long. Ultimately the lender will decide if they want to convert to the new credit scoring model, whether it is FICO 10 T, FICO 10, or both.

Reference Links

https://www.investopedia.com/terms/c/creditrating.asp

https://www.experian.com/blogs/ask-experian/credit-education/score-basics/credit-utilization-rate/

https://gradyfirm.wordpress.com/2016/04/11/why-is-it-so-important-to-establish-credit-in-the-us/

https://economictimes.indiatimes.com/wealth/invest/what-is-credit-rating-and-how-important-is-it-while-making-an-investment-decision/articleshow/65806143.cms?from=mdr

https://www.consumer.ftc.gov/articles/understanding-your-credit?

utm_medium=cpc&utm_source=google&utm_campaign=consumeredu&utm_content=bg-

05142020_CreditScore_YourCredit

https://www.cnbc.com/select/average-fico-score-hits-record-high-703/

https://www.experian.com/blogs/ask-experian/fico-10-score-changes-what-it-means-to-your-credit/

CHAPTER THREE: POVERTY MINDSET

"When you define your life by jealousy alone, you will never be able to come up with anything worthwhile to improve your condition."

HOW OFTEN HAVE YOU HEARD SOMEONE STATE THAT they can't make ends meet in spite of working hard, or that they will never be able to go on a vacation due to a lack of funds? Maybe you yourself have uttered these statements at some point in time. These are limiting thoughts that hamper your chances of success. There are several scientific studies confirming how thought patterns affect our general well-being and health. There are even pieces of evidence to suggest that negative thoughts might affect your immune system which in turn may lead to illness.

So why do people entertain these thoughts? After all, it is not easy to break out of a mold made of old habits. Perhaps you were raised in a household where you were constantly reminded of how limited your resources were and how the wealthy exploit the poor all the time. It is hardly surprising that one would carry such a mentality into adulthood. This kind of mindset is commonly known as a poverty mindset.

A person with a poverty mindset strongly believes that there is a scarcity of things in life. It is the mindset that it is hard to earn, things are hard to attain, and that there is not enough for everyone. This mindset is apparent in our actions, our words, and our thoughts. An example of a poverty mindset is buying cheap artificial butter which is not exactly a healthy choice when you can get organic butter by spending a few dollars more.

Living in a bad neighborhood for cheap rent is also an example of a poverty mindset. Individuals with such a mindset refuse to invest money in themselves because they want to save as much as they can.

People who are not able to gain wealth have small goals and small dreams. So if you tend to make do with what you got, can't imagine living a better life, find it difficult to come up with concrete plans, and are often aloof about personal development, you may have a poverty mindset. Lack of ambition can be attributed to a lack of encouragement in childhood which leads to low self-esteem due to which you attract the things that are not good for you and limit your potential.

To be honest, it is not always easy to deal with bad situations and it is normal to feel anger, sadness, and grief in these situations. These experiences can be educational and the emotions can propel you towards lessons that allow you to carve out a better future for yourself.

One of the most noticeable traits in a person suffering from poverty mentality is that they always place themselves in a helpless position. You may think of yourself as a victim with no control or power over what is happening with your life. This way, you wander around an endless cycle of pessimism, because you expect bad things to happen.

One of the other traits of poor mentality is intense jealousy. Such a person will always compare themselves with others, thinking they don't deserve what they have, and wanting those things for themselves. If you have a strong poverty mindset, you will be jealous of every other person and concentrate on this toxic feeling rather than what you want and what all are your strengths. When you define your life by jealousy alone, you will never be able to come up with anything worthwhile to improve your condition.

Another of the driving factors of the poverty mindset is, of course, fear. So even when you try to be assertive, you feel cornered. So rather than trying to obtain good things in life, you focus on protecting yourself and avoiding bad things. When you constantly live in fear, your body produces stress hormones, which traps you in an endless cycle of anxiety. So you never find time to unlock your true potential.

Even when you think about breaking the poverty mindset, your thoughts are naturally drawn to things that you lack. This lack makes you yearn for something else. However, this is not the right approach to coming out of the poverty mindset. This is because the jealousy factor comes into play here because when you always concentrate on what you lack, your attention is drawn to people who have all the possessions you care for. Thus, concentrating on what you lack is counterproductive as unbeknownst to you, more lack creeps into your life this way.

That being said, no matter how bad your situation is, you can break the poverty mindset if you are willing to self-reflect, focus, and put in some effort. The solutions to this problem involve changing daily habits and making use of advanced psychology techniques.

The first step to solving any problem is to confront it. Once you take a good, hard look at it, and recognize it for what it is, you can isolate it and stop agreeing with it. Often people get defensive when confronted about their shortcomings. This makes it harder for them to solve their issue because they are not ready to accept that the problem exists in the first place. So, you need to stop being defensive about your poverty mindset and not try to justify it.

Take a look at where you stand and ask yourself whether you would like to stay here. If you find yourself coming up with a positive answer, you must change your belief system as it is faulty. You must accept the fact that the absence of proper data is leading to intrusive thoughts and causing you to make some bad decisions in life.

Currently, our schools don't provide much education in terms of financial literacy. So you must educate yourself because your lack of knowledge makes it possible for others to take advantage of you. You should understand the basics of financial literacy, the options you have regarding financial institutions and products, how the concept of credit works and how you can build your own credit in a responsible way, and your rights when it comes to financial products and banking.

For example, if you are applying for a credit card for yourself, you should know about the Annual Percentage Rates (APR) that determines how much interest you'll need to pay in case you fail to make a payment. Before taking out a loan, you need to know about the repayment terms such as monthly payments and the duration of the loan, and the interest amount you owe. Lenders are duty-bound to tell you about the payment schedule and the total costs you'll incur because of the loan.

Just like we visit different stores to get the best deal while buying clothes and such, it is important that you shop around and consider your options before you choose a financial institution or a product. To a person belonging to a low-income bracket, it is vital to get the best deals and to save money wherever they can.

If you wish to enhance your knowledge about financial literacy, there are various online resources available for this purpose. You can also pay a visit to the Center for Financial Services Innovation (CFSI) which is a financial services consultancy that is known for helping out underbanked customers. You could also visit the Consumer Financial Protection Bureau (CFPB), an organization that makes sure financial institutions, lenders, and banks are treating you well. Here, you can join a program on financial education and coaching to increase your knowledge about finances.

For most people belonging to the low-income bracket, the principal challenge lies in changing the way they view money. Usually, the way a person is brought up plays a huge role in determining their attitude towards money. The first step to changing this mindset is to figure out your current financial condition and how you were raised in regard to money. You should ask yourself how your parents treated money and what common traits did you inherit from them.

You should also ask what causes you to spend money and how much money you owe, in total. Consider what little steps you can take in order to change your beliefs. Prominent financial educators talk about a particular mindset shift for under-privileged people. Instead of thinking of yourself as a poor person, you may think that you're just living with low wealth.

When you consider your situation as temporary, that gives you the power to change it. You realize that you have the mobility to change your income and reach a higher wealth status. You can do this by making smart financial decisions. Having the hope and confidence that things can be changed goes a long way when it comes to reclaiming your power in regard to your finances.

Of course, being hopeful and optimistic isn't enough. You need to take some real action if you truly wish to make things better for yourself. Mingle with people who are big thinkers, because the environment and the community will change your mindset for the better. Consult a financial mastermind who lives and thinks in abundance. It doesn't matter if you have a difference of opinions with them, because agreeing with everyone around you hasn't worked out too well, apparently, provided your financial condition is extremely poor.

You would need to pay for certainty and knowledge if you wish to devote time to yourself. Remember, fear is the driving force of poverty, so you should take part in courses that will enhance your financial knowledge, even if you're afraid to do it. A good rule to remember in this situation is that if you're scared of it, then you should definitely give it a try.

It makes no sense to struggle all by yourself. Your local community has many resources you can take advantage of. You need to think of them as an important step in improving your financial condition. Online resources are easily accessible and extremely helpful, although in some cases, there are no alternatives to a face-to-face discussion.

Some of the places where you can seek out financial education include community centers, churches, schools, public libraries, online and nonprofit organizations. If you wish to know more about taxes, you can always visit the IRS Tax Assistance Center. At these organizations, you will find programs that help you find the proper financial products that suit your needs, as well as helping you understand the basics of financial literacy, and how to complete your taxes.

You can opt for individual coaching sessions, courses, or attend the lectures of financial speakers. If you have more money to spend, you might get in touch with a legitimate financial adviser, counselor, or educator, and they can help you choose the right path.

The next steps involve the elimination of unhealthy financial practices, the chief among them being payday loans. It is a vicious cycle that seems innocuous at first but soon swallows you up, causing you to take loan after loan to clear your debts, thus making you spend the rest of your life paying back a single payday loan. We have already talked about payday loans earlier in this book, but it's important to mention it again in this context.

Millions of Americans take out payday loans every year and end up paying outrageous amounts as interest. For every $100 dollar borrowed, a payday loan would charge you somewhere between $10 to $30. So even if we consider the cost to be $15 per $100 borrowed, the APR comes out to be an outrageous 400%, whereas that of credit cards is about 12-30%. But not every person has access to credit cards, and they are forced to take out these predatory loans.

People mainly opt for these loans because they are in dire need of some immediate cash. It could also be that they are unaware of the other options that are available on the market, or they have bad credit ratings, which makes it difficult for them to access loans of higher quality with low-interest rates. So just aiming to avoid payday loans is not enough, since you might be forced into them due to your situation. You should also aim towards improving your credit score. This will give you access to favorable loans with reasonable interest rates that allows you to pay them back in full with little or no issues.

You don't always want to discuss your financial situation with friends and family, mostly because it can be a little awkward and even hurt your pride. But when you're in a bad situation, you need to shed these inhibitions and consult someone you know and trust who is good with money matters. This can be a great way to elevate yourself from poverty.

You can always learn from other people's experiences. Ask them questions regarding how they changed their financial situation, the things that worked out for them, and those that did not. Ask them questions regarding how to set up a budget and how they manage their expenditures. An outside opinion can be great as you can get valuable insight into factors you have never considered before.

Even if you don't know someone personally who is in finance, you could search online for an expert. These experts have extensive financial knowledge and personal experiences they can share with you. They can tell you about paying off your debts and improving your financial status through these experiences. If you don't have the time to have a face-to-face discussion, there are several podcasts and online videos where you can receive financial tips on the go.

You need to remember that you are not alone in this world, and there are plenty of people out there providing good advice, and plenty of resources that can help you get out of this dire situation you're in. I really want you to understand there is help available to you if you take the time and look for it!

Another important step to eliminating the poverty mindset is something that was touched upon earlier but wasn't discussed in detail. This is, of course, focusing on maintaining good credit for yourself. If you have bad credit, it limits your borrowing power, and you incur more costs in terms of insurance and interest rates. And not only this, but bad credit also impacts your career, as many companies do background verification of their employees before hiring them, and some of them check your credit score.

So in order to break the poverty cycle, you need to be more responsible about your credit. Depending on your situation, there are several ways you can go about rebuilding or establishing your credit. First of all, you need to figure out how credit functions and how they determine your credit score so that you can improve it. It isn't an instantaneous process and often takes several years. But by managing your credit well, you can access better loan terms, high-quality financial products, and more purchasing power, and hopefully, break the cycle of poverty.

Lastly, if you have your doubts regarding a financial institution or a product, you shouldn't be afraid to reject it. You should always walk away if the lender or bank seems to be withholding information and not being transparent in their dealings. There are plenty of options available for you when it comes to financial institutions so you should walk away while you still have the chance.

You have to remember that these financial institutions stand to profit from your association with them, and so you deserve to be treated with respect. This is a situation where you could ask for references from people you know and trust. Ask them if they've had good experiences with a particular institution before buying a financial product. It goes without saying that money is power, so you should invest it where you want to provide support and get support in return.

Remember, many financial organizations will claim to offer the best services, but in reality, there are many other options available for you. So you should do your own research to figure out what suits you best. By taking prudent financial decisions, creating assets, and managing your credit well, you can emerge out of the poverty mindset and transform your life.

Reference Links

https://medium.com/@jerryfetta/how-to-defeat-poverty-mindset-9ec6cb6b5407

https://www.inc.com/marla-tabaka/how-to-beat-the-poverty-mindset.html

https://www.nytimes.com/2017/05/30/upshot/ben-carsons-thinking-and-how-poverty-affects-your-state-of-mind.html

https://fee.org/articles/responsibility-is-the-antidote-to-the-poverty-mindset/

https://www.thelawofattraction.com/poverty-mindset-financial-abundance/

CHAPTER FOUR: BLUE COLLAR MINDSET

"People with such mindset are like athletes, who are able to go on in spite of the tiredness and the soreness."

A BLUE-COLLAR WORKER IS A PERSON BELONGING TO the working class who engages in manual labor, which may be skilled or unskilled in nature. Blue-collar workers can be found in areas in construction, mining, trucking, driving, waste collection, pest control, landscaping, logging, fishing, farming, operating power plants, electricity generation, warehousing, and manufacturing. It usually involves building or maintaining something.

They are often compared to white-collar workers who have desk jobs and are known to avoid physical labor or any kind. White-collar workers make more money than their blue-collar counterparts and while the former comfortably sits behind a desk, the latter has to get their hands dirty working in manufacturing or some other division. White-collar workers are also better educated than blue-collar workers and exist in a different social class.

A blue-collar worker often works on hourly wages or on a

contractual basis, where they get paid for every piece of an item they put together. Often, these workers form unions to maintain their job security and to ensure future work. They are often insecure about their job stability and often have to work on temporary jobs with no payment guarantee.

White-collar jobs, on the other hand, feature a strict and well-structured hiring process, because of which the people working these jobs are harder to fire. Although their income may sometimes depend on holding on to a client base, it is more stable than that of blue-collar workers as they have specific skills that they can put to use.

While these two job types are different in terms of duties and salaries, the line between the two worker types is fading day by day. With constant advancements made in technology, the education needed for blue-collar jobs is increasing, and so is the pay.

Blue-collar mindset refers to the typical mentality possessed by blue-collar workers where they know they have to get the job done, no matter what. This mindset is not limited to these classes of workers and in fact, all of us have it, more or less. It acts as a driving factor in our lives and allows us to wake up every morning, work for hours till the end, and not cry and complain because we don't feel appreciated enough.

In other words, a blue-collar mindset refers to the ability to put in maximum efforts even when you are not getting enough recognition. There is no award waiting for you and no bonus at the end of the year, but it doesn't matter. You have a stable job, and we are happy with it. But that does not mean, people with blue-collar mindsets don't get angry about their situation. They may change their beliefs and political views but that doesn't change the reality of getting up every morning, operating heavy machinery, or making that late-night truck run.

People with such mindset are like athletes, who are able to go on in spite of the tiredness and the soreness. They weld the pipes and swing the sickle because they know there is no other way, and if they stopped doing it, they would be betraying themselves. Even though they are not praised enough, they keep working because of their pride, and because they know they would not be doing something else instead.

In reality, the blue-collar mentality keeps society functioning, and without this mentality, the world will not be the same. We wouldn't put in the same amount of effort because of the lack of motivation. The ego, money, recognition, and pride that drives us will not be present, and so we will just stop working. The society would be filled with lawyers, doctors, and accountants, without anyone to do manual labor.

No society can function without these types of people or mindset because manual labor is quite necessary. Grinding is necessary. Going on even where there is no hope in sight is necessary, because someone has to do it. Without blue-collar workers, we would have no one to fix our cars, so they would disappear. Houses too will disappear since there would be no one to build and repair them, so we will be living in tents. And we would have to boil our water because there would be no plumbers.

So no matter how much the average blue-collar worker is mocked because of their coarse speech or rough behavior, without them, life would come to a standstill. But that being said, there is also a negative aspect to this mindset. People with the blue-collar mindset are often too deep into it, and they don't know where to stop with the daily grind. They start believing it is their fate to work on jobs like this and this often hinders their growth and stops them from exploring other options.

The blue-collar mindset can often be restricted in the sense that it can halt your learning process. You no longer believe in exploring new things and stop being curious. This is because you are afraid that considering other options might destroy the perfectly stable life you have built and so you keep on with the daily grind and go about your day in spite of the feeling of inadequacy pressing down upon you.

While the blue-collar mentality can limit the growth of an individual, it is sufficient to say that their mindset is something the rest of the society can learn from too. No, not the aspect of accepting and grinding and making no changes for a better future due to fear or even pride. But, there are some traits that the rest of the workforce can learn from the mindset of blue-collar workers.

Leadership skills are an important trait to have, especially if you are at the helm of an organization or if you are thinking of starting your own business. It is unwise to just assume that blue-collar workers are only useful for manual labor. Apart from their massive contribution to society, studying some aspects of their mentality and lifestyle will aid you to succeed in the world of business.

The greatest asset you can hone is honesty. This is the one area in which blue-collar workers exceed the white collars by miles. Being honest costs nothing but courage and conviction. While you might think that little white lies do not matter, but in the long run, they do. Once you have formed a habit of lying at the littlest things, the lies pile up, which ultimately leads to a disaster. It might be hard, to be honest, but that show of courage will not go unrewarded.

The transparency and honesty that you can integrate into a working environment will ultimately play a hand in the success of your organization. It is widely thought that white lies sustain a business, but in reality, nothing is better than honesty. If you are a business owner and you have complete honesty with your employees, then it is unlikely for them to hide anything from you.

This is critical for success as employees often hide or lie in the fear of getting fired or reprimanded. Their mistakes and not opening up about them at the correct time can lead to massive losses. About 89% of people stated that they value honesty in leaders. This statistic is highly indicative of the importance of honesty in working relationships.

The next thing that you can adopt from the blue-collar mentality is the work ethic that these workers possess. They are passionate about what they do, and this is reflected in their work and how much time and energy they invest in it. For the blue-collar workers, it is a matter of pride to show off how much they can work hard. Needless to say, if the rest of the workforce had a similar work ethic as the blue-collar workers, then the market and economy would change drastically.

This kind of work ethic is utterly significant and is a valuable trait needed in leaders. While it is true that the leaders needed to maintain a certain professional image, and as such grinding like others, on a daily basis is not an option. But, modifications of this work culture can be adopted. It is a sign of excellent leadership where you can claim and prove that you can go to extremes for your employees and business.

For that, you sometimes have to work till late at night or take over tasks that you think are not possible by a certain employee. This will not only boost your reputation among the employees but will also contribute to the success of your organization as a whole.

Having an exemplary moral code is another trait of the blue-collar workers that leaders must imbibe. Most of the blue-collar workers have strong moral beliefs, which are mainly due to the way they are brought up and the religion they practice. No matter the reason, this moral code aids them in attaining satisfaction and not doing anything that might come to nag their conscious sometime later.

This type of strong moral code, when adopted by the leaders, will help them to further their organization. This adoption of traits can manifest in numerous ways. You can do some social contributions by linking your organization to charities. Or you can also focus on uplifting the moral values of your employees. It is this moral code, that when displayed by leaders, invokes a specific passion and determination among employees that cannot be generated by anything else.

It is much more important to have an inspired employee that looks up to their leader than to have ones who are uninspired and could care less about the organization. Upholding the moral code can also help in cementing your good image among the employees. If the people who work with you are able to respect you without any stipulations, then you can motivate them to work harder.

The matter of the fact is people are more likely to be invested in your company if you are a good person. This is mainly because goodness is subconsciously liked and followed by people. Thus, by boosting respect and moral code among employees, you can drive them to do better and further the goals of your establishment.

Collaborative team effort is yet another trait that you can adopt from the blue-collar mentality. The majority of the blue-collar workers have strong communal ties and feel responsible for their families and the communities in which they live. This, in turn, influences their life and mentality.

To improve or boost the performance of employees, leaders are placed with the massive responsibility of facilitating open communication. When leaders stress that the goals of the organization and the results that are being achieved every day are due to a collaborative effort, it encourages and motivates the employees to work harder. It is vital that they feel a sense of belonging. Hence, it is extremely essential for leaders to organize scheduled meetings in order to remind the employees that the objective of the company can only be met by working together.

By observing such simple but effective traits and incorporating it, leaders in the white-collar market can further their goals and attain great success. It is futile to look down on the blue-collar workers when adopting some of their traits can do massive good for your business.

Reference Links

https://www.entrepreneur.com/article/337386
https://tempojournal.com/article/a-blue-collar-mentality/index.html
https://psychcentral.com/blog/blue-collar-roots-vs-white-collar-reality/
https://www.bucll.com/the-need-for-blue-collar/
https://dailyillini.com/special-sections/2020/01/27/rise-and-grind-mentality-doesnt-determine-success/

CHAPTER FIVE: MILLIONAIRE MINDSET

"How millionaires view money is indeed very different from how other people view money. Spending is just one aspect, separate from investments. Millionaire's want to hold on to their wealth, and for this, they start looking at things from a different perspective."

LOOKING AT THE ATTITUDE AND BEHAVIOR OF THE financially successful members of society and those who struggle to make ends meet, we notice some key differences. However, there is one particular trait that is common in both rich and poor, and that is the self-serving bias. This bias is a distortion of the perception present in an individual, where they ignore all the signs and still see themselves favorably.

We can notice this trait present in certain individuals coming from wealthy families who openly claim to be where they are purely due to their talent. Since most of us are not born with silver spoons in our mouths, it can be a bit frustrating to know about the lack of humility these people have.

Self-serving bias is a two-way street. Many people give more importance to luck while assessing the lives of successful people and underestimate the work ethic and talent that they have. Funny enough, when these people fail, we attribute it to a lack of talent rather than just plain bad luck.

There is a lesson we can learn from this. Luck is definitely a strong influencing factor in any outcome, but since none of us has control over luck, the only thing we can focus on is the mindset. By adopting a millionaire mindset, we can improve our chances of earning more wealth for ourselves. You will hear many renowned businessmen and industrialists saying that it is all about the mindset, and to a great extent, that is true.

Our minds can sometimes be capricious and undependable. Our opinions are constantly changing and this can make decision-making a confusing process. The millionaire mindset is characterized by a greater calling. It necessitates that we believe in something bigger than our present feelings, something that is not restricted to our worries and fears. Some people might argue as this being plain old intuition, while others may hold the opinion that they believe in their subconscious to lead them down the right path.

This mindset develops the way you work, act, and think in your personal and professional life. It involves getting rid of confounding, unhealthy, and negative characteristics and developing creativity, sound health, focus, and discipline. When you put in so much effort to think strategically, it pervades every corner of your life.

You adopt the habits of creating goals for yourself and planning out strategies to achieve your goals. You set a timeline and educate yourself, working hard, and letting your creativity show you the way.

One of the chief characteristics of a millionaire mindset is spending your time on things you don't pay much attention to, normally. You might start taking yoga classes, learn how to sew, play bridge, learn chess, or a musical instrument. In both your personal and professional life, you will find that you are able to move out of your comfort zone with relative ease. All of your actions will be influenced by this new mindset and its characteristics.

You will turn into this person people look up to, and love to be around. In other words, you will become infinitely more interesting. You will notice some people in your circle drifting away, and that is alright. When you are surrounded by people who spend so much time on wasted efforts, it is hard to gain better life skills.

You will start attracting hard-working and smart people who realize that there is more to life than spending money. Even though initially you might have wanted to become a millionaire simply to buy anything you wanted, you will find that after becoming one, your mentality has changed. You will turn into a brand new person, and if you did this through dedication and honest work, you will become a better person, hopefully.

Before a person decides to adopt the millionaire mindset, they might have had a decent job, or they might have been homeless. But all of these people had one thing in common, they were not happy with their prior situation. To rewire your brain, work hard, and cease unnecessary expenditures demands a person be prepared to relinquish their current practices and bring out a drastic change in their life.

People want to become wealthy for different reasons, however, when they reach the point where they have a million dollars in their bank accounts, they are reaping the benefits of their hard work, developed an excellent work culture, and have bolstered their wisdom with money. At this point, their lifestyle is such that the wealth keeps on accumulating, so they have the time to pursue other interests.

As you let the millionaire mindset control every aspect of

your life, you learn that it is not so much about the goal as it is about the process. When you live your life to the fullest, you are filled with energy and contentment, and you feel a connection with similar people living in different corners of the world. When you follow your true calling, step out of your comfort zone, work hard, and make excellent decisions, you find out that there is more to life than you ever realized.

It is no secret that the personal life of wealthy people is quite different from others. Some millionaires hang on to their thrifty lifestyles, some openly fault it, while others go on a mad spending spree. The outcome depends on whether you spent time creating a focused mindset and good characteristics. If you want to earn a lot of money just to throw it all away with uncontrolled investment and spending, then you must ask yourself, what was the point of earning that wealth? If you wish to be a millionaire for the rest of your life and not just a fleeting moment, then it requires a great deal of discipline and commitment.

You can be a person who leads a disciplined life and still own a yacht, a luxury car, and a palatial house, but here we must consider the upkeep that these things take. In order to maintain expensive things, you need to pay more in terms of upkeep. If you are focused from the get-go and have the right mindset and character, you will spend wisely, keeping in mind your future investments.

Very often you see someone inheriting a lot of money and then losing it all, as they did not inherit the mentality needed to manage such a vast quantity of wealth. Any self-made millionaire will tell you the kind of discipline and hard work it takes to accumulate that much wealth. You will always find them behaving in a way that shows how much they value the money that they earned.

A research conducted on American millionaires revealed that they have developed such a discipline that their lifestyles do not change even after they have earned so much wealth. Since they worked to reach their point, by being prudent and sensible with their spending, they cannot overnight become spendthrifts.

Many millionaires live in much less luxury than they could, which means that they don't always live in a mansion, drive around in a luxury car, or dress differently from the common folk. Often millionaires follow a frugal lifestyle, which is why you hear about people who die and leave millions of dollars to charity, even though their lifestyle never revealed that they had that kind of money.

If you've let go of your bad habits, love what you do, and live a healthy life, your personality will reflect that. You will have friends with the same mentality, and instead of referring to you as a millionaire, they will say great things about you as a person. If you have successfully established your own business or rose to the very top of your organization by being careful with your money, you simply don't quit your habits once you get there.

The way you molded yourself to reach your goal becomes who you are. It becomes an integral part of you. While other people try and convince themselves into buying something, a person with a millionaire mindset will know it is better sometimes to keep the money inside the wallet. Adopting this mindset will lead to habits that will dictate your decisions and they in turn will dictate your life.

Most people don't develop a millionaire mindset when they are young, but that doesn't mean it is unheard of. If you are one of those people who like to spend more and work less, people around you might think you are rich. But someone with a millionaire mindset realizes that to be rich, you need to take a different path and to remain rich you need to adopt a different lifestyle. At any point in your life, you can lead this change and think as a millionaire does.

Whether you are young or old doesn't matter. A millionaire mindset can be adopted by a person who lives a comfortable life, and by someone who struggles to earn their daily wage. All it comes down to is how badly you want that life. Today there are a great number of opportunities for someone to go down this path, but the competition is tougher and the path is rougher than ever before. Because of this, you need to decide your destination, both in terms of professional and personal life.

Take a good, hard look in the mirror and ask yourself who you are. Do you like who you are? Or do you want to be something much more? It is not always about money, although that is the chief motivating factor. It is about living a better life, where you can be content and happy, and where you can help those who are in need. You can either lift people up or let them drag you down. There are no two ways about it.

Separating business from pleasure is not something that millionaires do. If you are passionate about your work, then your business and your pleasures are one and the same. Yes, there will be some struggle in the beginning, but if you've got your strategies planned, are concentrating on expanding the boundaries of your mind, and striving to learn new and interesting things, you will reach the point where you can see beyond what lies immediately in front of you.

This accomplishment will be the inspiration that you need to keep going. A millionaire wakes up every day, excited and ready to tackle whatever comes along their way. This is not because he has no work to be done, but because they get the chance to do what they love. What that thing is, is irrelevant. In every business, you will find millionaires.

So what makes a millionaire different from someone who struggles throughout their lives trying to do better? It depends on how strong your foundation is. You have to comprehend how your mind functions, let go of bad habits and work on building disciplined, healthy, and positive characteristics. You can only come up with a strategy once you figure out how your mind works.

Some people are raised in such an atmosphere that strategic thinking comes to them naturally. If in a family, the parents practice strategic thinking, then it is expected the children will get a headstart. In these families, the children too are expected to set goals and plan out strategies for reaching them. These parents realize that through this process, you can carve out a meaning for yourself, and that is what they want the child to work towards.

Strategic thinking that influences every little aspect of life. It influences their decisions when it comes to work, play, budget, and shopping. Some of them use gift coupons, purchase second-hand cars, and even shop at thrift stores, thus leading a frugal life. If you spend money faster than you make it, then soon there will be nothing left in your bank. You will end up feeling awful about yourself, having thrown away all the money you worked so hard to earn, but more importantly, you will have shifted your focus on the more important things in life, and splashing money around to your heart's content is no longer so tempting.

How millionaires view money is indeed very different from how other people view money. Spending is just one aspect, separate from investments. Millionaire's want to hold on to their wealth, and for this, they start looking at things from a different perspective. If there is an entity through which their wealth is getting drained, then it must be stopped. If you wish to maintain your wealth, you cannot continue with your bad habits, your car and house expenses, and your loan interest amounts.

This is the outlook millionaires have towards life. Those people who have a negative mindset and those who practice unhealthy living are those you need to let go of. As you progress through life, you need to stop and examine what you're doing. This will allow you to invest in both your personal and professional lives. The real goal is not being a millionaire but is one for the remaining part of your life.

One of the striking qualities of millionaires is their diverse range of interests. A millionaire's passion is not restricted. You will find millionaires in rice farming, pest control, real estate, construction, junk, lawn care, inventing, and speaking. It doesn't matter what kind of work they do. What makes you content, excited, and creative is worth finding. Take a good look at yourself and study where you spend most of your time. That is what you love doing, and you will shine if you seek out careers in that department. It is through passion and hard work that people become millionaires, not through the career.

Sometimes you can make a major discovery just by being observant and creative. You see a necessity, something that is dysfunctional and can be made better. You see a thing that, if it had a new purpose, would be more fun. Creative can act as a fuel for your energy and your brain, but to get wealthy, there is no alternative to working hard while being focused and disciplined.

So how do you start thinking like a millionaire? The first thing you should remember is that looks can be deceiving. We all have mental images when it comes to millionaires, and they usually involve luxury mansions, sports cars, helicopters, etc. Many non-millionaires feel that you need to spend your money freely in order to display your status and your worth. But this is a wrong notion, as many millionaires follow a budget and lead frugal lives so as not to waste money buying unnecessary things.

If you are finding it difficult to separate the idea of being wealthy from the temptations attached to it, spend some time thinking and consider why these status symbols are so important. Is there really any need to impress someone with an expensive watch or a new car? What would you rather have? A Lamborghini and an empty bank account, or the car's worth of money in the bank?

Most people believe there is a purpose to their lives, some specific reason why they were put on earth. Millionaires perceive their roles in life quite differently from others. Psychologists believe that there are two internal loci of control, internal and external, which determines how people perceive the degree of control they have over their own lives. Millionaires have an internal locus of control.

People with an internal locus of control perceive themselves as leading their own lives. For example, if such a person had a failed investment, they would not blame the circumstances, luck, or other people, as they would reevaluate the process to find out where they went wrong, thus learning from their mistake.

In contrast, a person with an external locus attaches too much importance to external factors, and they feel like whatever is happening with their lives is inevitable and there is no way they can change it. If they made the same failed investment, they would think that they couldn't have prevented it, and that luck was not on their side that day. So while an investor with an external locus would stop with his investments after failing for the first time, one with an internal locus would get themselves back into the game with brand new insights.

Changing your locus of control is a monumental task. Blaming fate, God, or the circumstances is easy because then when you fail, you have no obligation to keep pushing and keep trying. But if you wish to accumulate a vast amount of wealth like a millionaire, you need to realize that you alone have the power to realize your dream.

The millionaire mindset also involves taking calculated risks. You may think that taking out a personal loan and starting your own business when you already have a stable job is not a smart move. But that decision might be what stands between you becoming a millionaire, and you struggling to earn your daily bread. You need to let go of the scarcity thinking and embrace rich thinking.

Your current job may be the safe option, but if you wish to become a millionaire, you must set bigger goals for yourself. If you don't take these risks, then you can never improve your current condition and create not only wealth but a meaning for yourself.

To let go of the fear, you need to ask yourself a few questions. Ask yourself what are the best and worst outcomes of your decision. What is the most likely outcome? At the time when an opportunity presents itself, the answers to these questions can provide you with some much-needed insight.

If the most favorable outcome will take you nearer to your goal and if you are prepared to face the worst outcome if it comes to that, then you should take action and make that choice. Those with a scarcity mindset feel any risk to be too high, and that means they can never reach the point of accumulating wealth for themselves.

Wishing for something is not the hard part. People wish for a better job, a better house, a better body, etc. But very few of these half-hearted wishes ever gets converted to reality. You must know about or seen firsthand how people buy diet books and lottery tickets while never actually reaching their goals.

If you always lament about your lack of wealth, you're not taking any action to reach your goals. While people around you are building for the future, you are wasting time with wishful thinking. Millionaires know that they have to commit themselves to wealth, and not just think about getting wealthy overnight.

One simple technique many people use it to write down your goals on a piece of paper. It helps you achieve clarity and also gives you the time you need to think about how to go on about achieving them. To enhance your odds of reaching your goal, you can imagine a world where your problems are solved and then think about the bad aspects of reality that you have to deal with. This will encourage you to take responsibility and chalk out actionable plans.

Millionaires, when they purchase something, think of it as an asset they can later sell for a good return. In other words, they always look for a return on investment or ROI. It is the amount of value returned on investment, taking into account the cost of investment. These smart buys and invest-ments are what sets them apart from others.

Making smart investments doesn't always involve the stock market. You need to figure out which investments are ideal for you. This could mean opening a money market or IRA account or taking your 401(k) account to the maxi-mum. You should make your money work and not keep all of your savings in static accounts. You don't have to invest a large amount, and you can start with one you're comfortable with.

While the blue-collar mindset involves planning for each year, millionaires often plan a decade ahead and work towards a goal they want to reach within 10 years. They create different streams of income so that the cash keeps flowing and the wealth keeps on building. Many of them resort to self-funding towards the beginning of their careers and slowly work their way upwards. So you see, self-funding is not a crazy idea. With a proper mindset, hard work, and determination, anyone can do it.

Reference Links

https://www.keepinspiring.me/secrets-of-a-millionaire-mindset/
https://www.universalclass.com/articles/self-help/the-millionaire-mindset.htm
https://www.entrepreneur.com/article/306652
https://www.lifehack.org/articles/money/develop-millionaire-mindset-6-easy-steps.html
https://medium.com/swlh/millionaire-mindset-6-steps-to-behave-like-a-millionaire-e1a0f2225980

CHAPTER SIX: TRULY UNDERSTANDING YOUR ASSETS AND LIABILITIES

"It is important to keep in mind that both time and money, once spent, cannot be regained."

THE PATH TO OBTAINING ECONOMIC SECURITY, IF NOT excess, is based on some basic financial education that is utterly important. This education comprises identifying the basic difference between assets and liabilities. You must think that people with even a little bit of financial knowledge would be able to understand it. However, that is not true.

The education that one receives is mostly through accountants or books related to finance. Often, these sources offer you information through financial jargon that undoubtedly goes over your head. To simplify it in layman terms, assets are anything that can provide you with money. It is basically what you own and has value. Whereas liabilities are those things that cause you to give out money. It is the money that you owe.

For a detailed understanding of what assets you have, you need to make a list of all the items that you think can be of value. Cash, any type of deposits or funds that you have made in a bank, mutual funds, and stocks are all assets. Even your retirement account and life insurance are counted as assets. Vehicles, personal belongings of value, real estate, and money that you have given to someone are also various types of assets.

In order to fully get a grasp of your financial situation, it is not enough to only make a list of your assets. You must also compile a list of your liabilities so that you can work towards eliminating them steadily. But, identifying them is a crucial step. Any payment or debt has to be counted as a form of liability. Any type of loan, including home equity loan, student loan, personal loan, automobile loan, etc. are liabilities. Even the mortgage of your house and your credit card debt are liabilities.

Even after the identification of assets and liabilities is done, it is normal to have confusion. There are several things that you may view as an asset but is actually a liability. For example – it is natural that you consider your house as an asset. After all, you have put in tremendous efforts and money to make sure that you gain some profit from it in the future. But, more often than not, your house becomes a major liability. The fact that you have to pay mortgages, insurance, taxes, and even maintain it – all points towards it being a liability. The only way that it can turn into an asset is if you can sell it for a profitable amount in the future. The chances of this happening are, to be honest, quite low.

The clear understanding of assets and liabilities allows you to look for or take up opportunities that can ultimately lead to being an asset. It is important to keep in mind that both time and money, once spent, cannot be regained. Sure, you must be thinking that you can just earn more money, right? Yes, that is absolutely true! With determination, patience, talent, and a little bit of luck, you can easily earn more money. But, this money does not negate the amount that you have already spent.

You might also think that you have a lot of time to achieve your dreams and that there is no hurry. There is no correct answer to this thought. It is a mixture of a yes and a no. Yes, you do have time, especially if you are young, but you also do not have any way of knowing what challenges or difficulties that you might face the very next day. This is why it is so very important to create such opportunities that will ultimately be profitable for you.

Many of us are born with inherent skills, and then, there are some that we develop over time. But, the question is not whether you have any skill or not. In fact, the question that you must ponder over is if you can recognize those skills and turn them into an asset for yourself.

For instance, if you have a knack or interest in computer languages or simply working with computers, then that is a skill. Now, what you can do is sharpen that skill by receiving an appropriate education. This way you can utilize your love for computers and skills in computing and earn a degree, or certificate which will later help you in getting a job. Or you are good at dancing. This is a skill that you can develop to be an asset. You must get the proper training required along with a certificate that proves your merit. With the aid of the certifications and experience that you have, you can get a job in the field of dance.

But, to turn the skills into an asset, you must be aware of the talents that you have. Sometimes, it is possible that you do not understand or give much importance to the skill that you possess. It is vital that you make a list of what you can do and then conduct extensive research to see how these skills might benefit you in the long run. Keep in mind that anything that aids you in earning money is an asset.

Understanding what opportunities might have a positive

impact on your self-development or business is crucial. It is important to identify these opportunities and then act on them immediately. Often, we take too much time and over-think, which leads us to lose some lucrative opportunities.

Often, hobbies are perceived as a getaway from the stress of our daily lives. It is not unlikely to seek a few minutes of peace or satisfaction while indulging in some hobby. However, you can also consider the fact that turning a hobby into a business opportunity is not necessarily a bad idea. If you carefully research your hobby and estimate its demand in the market, you can easily conclude if turning your hobby into a business will bring in some profits or not.

For example- If you have a penchant for photography and the idea of capturing time in a frame and immortalizing it intrigues you, then you can consider turning it into a business. You can put some of your works on your website or Facebook page and interact with your friends and family to let them know that you are seeking potential clients. You start slow, take on a few clients, and the trick to make a name for yourself is to prove your worth before charging the amount you think you deserve. That means, initially you might have to charge a little less, but you can consider it as a payment for marketing. As your business grows, you can charge more and continue.

Part-time jobs can also be converted to a full-fledged business. You need to make sure that you have time, the money needed, and the means to market it. For example – You love to cook, and therefore, work for a few hours as a chef in a restaurant. After some experience and popularity, you can set up your own restaurant. Keep in mind that it is not going to be easy, and you may think that you are way over your head. When this happens, take a deep breath and remind yourself why you wanted to do this in the first place. Owning a business will ultimately earn you money, and if maintained carefully, can be an asset of a lifetime for you.

For a business to flourish or even take off, it is important that you are efficient in managing time. In today's world, where time is not given the utmost importance and is spent almost carelessly, it is vital that you are aware of how critical it is to utilize time for your own benefit. Most of the time, you tend to spend time indulging in things that have no real value and do not contribute even a little bit towards the goal that you have envisioned.

For instance – Spending an hour or more for scrolling mindlessly through social media or talking with friends via message or call. Now you must be thinking that is it so wrong to spend some time on some respite or simply maintaining a social life? After all, no one wants to be an outcast. It is absolutely fine to spend a few minutes talking with others and taking a break.

But, if you are not aware of the time spent, then that few minutes could easily lead up to an hour, then two hours, and before you know, you have just spent an entire day doing absolutely nothing fruitful. Only after the day is spent, do you realize that you could have utilized it to complete the outline of your business project. But, the time gone can never be regained, and this is exactly why managing time and utilizing it is so important.

There are several ways that you can manage time. The foremost thing that you can do is to make a schedule for the day. It is very simple to do now with your mobile phone. I personally set up my weekly schedule using the calendar on my phone. In this schedule, allocate the tasks, and during the day, you must strive to complete the tasks before the day ends. Remember to not over-expect. This means that you must not burden yourself with a lot of tasks and subconsciously set yourself up for failure. It is better to have few tasks, manage it within a particular time frame, and then increase the number of tasks slowly.

In order to make sure that you are not wasting time, you need to work on identifying the time killers. No, these are not like the ones that the law officials are trained to catch. But, these are just as potent as them. Time killers can be defined as those activities that do not contribute towards the fulfillment of your objective or dream but simply work to waste the valuable time that you have.

Determination of these time killers are absolutely essential as eliminating them can offer you time that you never even thought that you had. This includes binge-watching your favorite television or web series on Netflix, spending a large portion of the day (almost as much as 40% of your day) on scrolling through YouTube, or just going through different social media platforms, etc.

To make it easy for you to recognize time killers, you can go through the ones that are mentioned here. But, recognizing them is not enough. You must also take the necessary steps to curb them. This might seem like an impossible task due to familiarity and addiction, but with enough determination, nothing is impossible, right?

The foremost time killer is email. Now, the most obvious question that is bound to pop up is how can searching or going through emails be something that is equivalent to wasting time? Checking your emails is not a time killer, but checking it constantly is. To make sure that you do not form a habit, it is better to schedule your readings, and only check it out of schedule when it's absolutely necessary. Another thing that you can do is remove all sorts of notifications, including audio and visual that will constantly nag you to open it.

It might come as a huge surprise, but meetings are also great time killers. Now, confusion over this particular statement is evident. But, what this statement means is that there are some meetings, which are absolutely unnecessary but still you have to be present because you are asked to. If you are attending a meeting that you feel might not be beneficial for you in any way, you can discuss it with your seniors respectfully. Now, if you are leading the meeting, then you need to call the ones that are directly involved or affected by the contents of the meeting. There is no use involving everyone and wasting their time.

Next is the endless surfing of the internet. Now, it is true that watching some funny videos or reading an article might help you feel refreshed, but it is vital that you keep track of the time that you are investing. To be honest, a few minutes are fine, but when it extends to a whole day, it is time to do something about this obvious addiction. You must be firm and keep yourself from scrolling the internet. If you can keep yourself busy during the time you usually spend on the internet, then you can get rid of this temptation.

Often, we tend to waste time that can easily be used to do something productive. The time that is spent traveling can be taken advantage of. For example – if you use public transport, it is not possible for you to make an important call, but this is the perfect opportunity for you to respond to some urgent messages, or you can watch videos that will ultimately aid you in reaching your goal. However, if you have a car, you can utilize this time to make calls. But, make sure that you are safe and do not text while driving. By doing so, you are not only putting yourself but others at risk too.

Now, procrastination is something that is quite common, right? Sometimes, we don't feel like doing certain tasks. This leads to the delay of the task from being completed and wastage of time. You might think that the time spent procrastinating is not much, but when you actually count it up, you will be surprised to see that it is in fact, **a lot.** There are no easy solutions to prevent you from procrastinating. One thing that you can do whenever you feel lazy or lose interest in doing a task is to remind yourself about why the task is important or what you can do after the task is done and you are free.

Non-business conversations or any such conversations that do not contribute towards your goal are a time killer. It is impractical to even state these conversations must not happen. Human beings are social creatures, and as such, interaction with others, the informal ones, are necessary for survival. The best solution that you can have for this particular time killer is not removing it, but rather reducing it. You can work on reducing the amount of time that you talk with others about nothing substantial. This way, you get to have a social life and work towards your goal at the same time.

Only by acknowledging the fact that time and money both wasted can never be regained, can you work towards curbing time killers and creating or finding opportunities that will help you to build assets. Keep in mind that the rich do not retain their wealth simply by indulging in luxury or using their talents. It is mainly because they are aware of how to handle their assets and work diligently on removing liabilities as soon as possible.

CHAPTER SEVEN: MILLIONAIRE MINDSET FOR THE BLUE-COLLAR WORKER

"In most cases, blue-collar workers are so involved in living in the present that they forget about the future."

AS ELABORATED IN A PREVIOUS CHAPTER, BLUE-COLLAR workers are mainly used to describe people who have professions that require manual labor. Can you imagine being a blue-collar worker and working towards becoming a millionaire? The question might leave you baffled, but it is indeed quite possible to achieve that improbable dream by simply developing a millionaire mindset.

Most of the self-made millionaires that you know today owe their wealth, success, and fame to a particular mindset. A certain way of thinking and then enacting those thoughts pave the way to achieve greatness in terms of wealth.

You might be harassed with a plethora of condescending questions ranging from "You are just a construction worker, and you think you can become a millionaire?" to "By working in a warehouse, you expect to get rich?" It is natural to feel embarrassed or even humiliated. But, statistics suggest that it is the blue-collar workers that have more chances of becoming rich. Without college debt hanging on your head, it becomes much easier to make critical financial decisions.

Early savings coupled with compound interest can give you a great head start towards superior financial status when compared with college-goers. Moreover, with the high demand for numerous blue-collar jobs, it is not fanciful to state that their earnings are much more than those earned with a college degree.

Putting aside misconceptions, false notions, and prejudices, you must determine your money mindset. This term may surprise you but is rather simple to grasp. In most cases, blue-collar workers are so involved in living in the present that they forget about the future. This could cost you a lot, including massive debts that will take years for you to pay it off. The first thing that you must do is develop a suitable money mindset. This is obviously easier said than done.

Often, you buy or purchase things that you think are valuable or trendy or simply because others also have it. This does bring joy for some time, but the regrets and the money that has cost you come to haunt you after some time. This miserable feeling deters you from actually enjoying the thing you bought. So, an important question needs to be asked before purchasing anything. Ask yourself if buying that particular thing would provide a sense of freedom? Or, will the purchase of that thing bring you peace and improve your life in any way?

The honest answer that you can give yourself will allow you to determine if buying the things that ultimately lead you to incur liabilities is worth it or not. After you developed a much realistic approach and are clear about your goals, you will find that investing in things that actually aid you in inching towards your goal is not that hard.

The foremost principle that encompasses the millionaire mindset is that you have to be willing to work hard. You must take that extra mile that ordinary people often do not. It is this extra step that will advance you from others. Whenever you feel lazy on a Sunday evening or do not wish to work at 4 am on a cold winter, it is important to remind yourself that only by hard work and sheer will can you achieve your dream of becoming a millionaire.

Another thing that you need to keep in mind is that you must work out a plan. This does not mean that you have to make a detailed, concrete plan immediately. But, the more quickly you start on a plan, the more you can alter it accordingly. You must have a vision for your future. It is important to start with small goals, but remaining stuck there just because of its comfort and familiarity is not ideal.

After accomplishing small goals, it's time to dream big and outline it in a detailed plan. Ask yourself, where do you want to be when you retire? Or, what do you want to do after walking away from a job that you did for 30 years? Even selling your business to someone else and living off of that money requires deliberation and planning. Impulsiveness is a trait that you have to curb. It is vital to remember that millionaires do not make impulsive decisions, mostly because decisions stemming from impulsiveness often end up being regrets.

Another aspect of developing a millionaire mindset is to accept changes and adapt accordingly. It is futile to hold onto beliefs and assumptions that were true 20 or 30 years ago. With the world changing its pace so often, it is highly important to keep up. The other alternative is to remain behind and live an ordinary life filled with regrets and what-ifs. You must grasp the concept that with time changing, opportunities change too. This is why it is important to take professional financial advice before making any major decisions.

You might think that you are knowledgeable about it, but your information or knowledge is bound to be a speck when compared to that of a professional. Searching for new financial opportunities is a great way to become a millionaire, but you must be willing to accept advice and then make a sound decision.

The people that you seek financial advice need not be restricted to professionals. It is vital to building up a team that will aid you in fulfilling your vision. This means interacting with others and making them believe in your dream. This team can have varied members ranging from family to friends to business partners and even associates. You must also take the advice of your mentors, if any, seriously. Having such a team to back you up will not only prevent you from costly mistakes but will also encourage you to go on even when you feel that it is absolutely impossible.

On your quest to become a millionaire, it is evident that you heard numerous people saying that you have to be willing to work hard. But does working hard mean working harder? This is a question that is bound to raise confusion and even some laughs. What does this even mean? It means that the concept of working hard does not indicate that you have to put yourself into the ground while doing so. You might be able to understand it a little better with an example.

For instance, one man making a 1000 cold calls all by himself is an example of working very hard. But the same man with a team of 10 people making those 1000 cold calls is an example of hard work. Understanding this difference might make things easier for you. Building a team and sharing your vision with them not only helps you make your vision a reality but also assists you to look into other areas. Delegating work and trusting other team members to do their part is a sign of excellent leadership. These leadership skills are imminent when it comes to becoming a millionaire.

Utilizing other people's time and talent for your vision or project is utterly essential. It is important to know all you can about the people that might be of any significance to your project. This information will allow you to have the leverage that you need to attain their skill and precious time for your quest. For finding out the leverage, it is vital that you study the person in detail. Only after you know sufficient things about them, can you make a move or offer that they cannot refuse.

But, having a millionaire mindset is not sometimes enough for blue-collar workers. Despite not having student loans, there are massive possibilities of a variety of other loans that you might need to pay off. Most people may be unaware of the fact that tradelines can be used to pay off any type of debt, which can extend to a house loan, car loan, student loan, etc.

However, to obtain a large credit limit amount, you must have an excellent credit score. There is no other way for you to get a big loan. But, now the question of how to establish a good credit score arises. Often, you buy things on a credit card and pay it way later. This is not good for your credit score and will ultimately hamper your chances of gaining a much-needed loan.

Now, how to establish a good credit score? The easiest way to do this is to open a retail card as they can be obtained with relative ease. The stores are more likely to give you an option to pay you in cash, but here lies in the opportunity for you to open a credit card. Now, after any purchase, try it to pay it off with this credit card. The sooner you pay, the more you increase your chances of having credit. Now that you have credit, you can apply for a credit card. But, make sure to use the card to purchase items that you can pay off immediately. Now that you have established a great credit rating, you can apply for a big loan or mortgage with ease.

Have you ever thought of being able to pay off a mort-gage under a period of 6 years? Impossible right? But, simple mathematics and some expert financial aid can turn this fanciful notion into a reality. Imagine the possibilities that you can achieve if you are able to pay off a debt meant for 30 years, incurring a massive amount of interest within a mere 6 or 7 years. This might also help you to gain some wealth in real estate.

Without the worry of debt, life becomes easy, and you have more clarity to focus on your quest of becoming a millionaire. Being able to pay off a massive debt can easily lead you to live a lifestyle that you have always imagined but actually never thought possible.

For instance, you have taken a loan amount of $180,000 as a mortgage for your house. The annual interest rate that is usually levied is 5%, and the total amount plus the interest incurred is to be paid back within a maximum period of 30 years. Let's say that the starting date of the loan is 1st January 2018. With a scheduled payment of monthly $966.28 (this amount is the principal added along with the interest), you incur total interests of an amount of $167,860.41.

This simple mathematical calculation is enough to raise your blood pressure levels. With interest amounting to almost the amount of loan taken, it is no wonder that most people spent a major portion of their life paying off the debts.

However, with the use of several funding instruments some financial advisors call "debt weapons", you can significantly cut down the number of interests while also being able to pay off the loan within a short span of 5-7 years. By using your home equity lines of credit or unsecured lines of credit, you can arrange for a lump sum, which will ultimately aid you in clearing your debt sooner.

During the first monthly payment of $966.28, if you can pay a hefty sum of $24,000, then you have the chance to save a lot of money in the form of interest. With savings and some careful financial calculations, it is not that hard to secure the $24,000 that is needed. Even if you borrow the amount, then the total interest that you would have to give is an additional $1000, which is significantly less. The extra payment of $24,000 has helped you save a total interest of $64,897.66. Due to this huge amount that you made at the first payment, you can save up on the area of total interest. The total interest now lowers down to $103,844.63.

Then, you continue to pay the amount scheduled for the entire year. After exactly one year, on 1st December 2018, you must make the same additional payment of $24,000. After this second hefty payment, you save up future interest amounting to $101,773.23. This way, you can save up a lot of interest. By the third $24,000 payment, you save interest amounting to $124,154.62. After the fourth payment, the total interest saved becomes $136,873.22. On the fifth payment, the interest saved is predicted to be $142,827.87.

With the last payment of $24,000 on 1st December 2022, the amount to be paid back is lowered to under $1700.00. Almost the entire mortgage amount is paid back under 5 years. The $24,000 is now being paid back along with the $966.28 principal interest payment that you do not have to pay for the mortgage anymore. This means that the $24,000 instead of being paid back in 12 months, will be paid back just within 8.

So, within 5 years and 8 months, a total amount of $144,917.40 interest can be saved along with the cut down of 299 future payments.

This example shows you how it is entirely possible to pay off a huge amount taken as a loan by the use of debt weapons. Now, questions may come to your mind as to what are debt weapons? Debt weapons can be a variety of things, but it is essentially the use of several lending products to apply a lump sum amount towards any kind of debt (Mortgage, car loan, student loan, etc.). The use of debt weapons is an ingenious way to pay back a loan within a very short time frame.

For example, you take an account and borrow a lump sum amount. Then, you use this lump sum to make an early payment to another loan, and it instantly cuts off 5 or even 6 years of payments of that particular loan. When your paycheck comes in, and you park it against the debt weapon instead of the savings or checking account, this strategy is termed as paycheck parking. Now, paycheck parking can be done against checking or saving accounts too, but the benefit you get from doing it against the debt weapon balance is that it reduces the daily average balance of that particular account throughout the entire month.

Only by using all the financial weapons and listening to sound advice, can anyone work towards the path of becoming a millionaire. To be honest, it is not a very far-fetched concept. But, to accomplish it, one needs to shed or simply shrug off the old-school knowledge and embrace the world as it is now. With the world changing so much, it is only apt that you change accordingly and adopt the new financial paths. This is also one of the many reasons millionaires are what they are today. They follow sound financial advice and then make a decision which aids in furthering their finances in a positive direction.

CHAPTER EIGHT: TRADITIONAL SELF-FUNDING OPTIONS AND LOANS

"..taking out a loan you will struggle to repay could tie you down to a boring job and force you to make compromises by passing up better job opportunities."

WHEN IT COMES TO SELF-FUNDING, MANY PEOPLE consider borrowing from their 401(k) plans, although financial advisers consider it to be a bad idea. Some plan holders use hardship provisions to draw money from their accounts, but they are more likely to borrow money temporarily. The loans may seem tempting, since you can borrow 50% of the amount you invested, up to $50,000 for a period of 5 years. There is no tax for this loan as you only borrow the funds, not withdraw them. Then you must gradually repay the loan, in both interest and principal.

401(k) loans have low-interest rates when compared to personal loans. Moreover, the interest goes to you instead of the lender or the bank. So, you are essentially paying yourself back for using your money. Therefore, some financial counselors endorse these loans, especially for people who do not have other options available. However, many of them advise against this practice, stating that it is not a good financial practice for the long-term.

Once you realize how you need to pay back the money you have borrowed, this type of loan becomes questionable. You need to remember that you deposited pre-tax money to your 401(k) account, but when you pay yourself back, you will be using after-tax money. For example, if you belong to the 24% tax bracket, you get 76 cents for every $1 earned, and the rest you must pay as income tax. So, in this tax bracket, you must put in 25% more effort to make your funds complete again, than what you did for the original deposit.

Although you can get a low-interest rate by borrowing from your 401(k), it is balanced out by the fact that there is no investment return. It is a common assumption that 401(k) loans cost nothing because you are paying the interest back to yourself. But there is a loss of opportunity in terms of potential earnings. The funds you borrowed can no longer grow now, and if such an account has a yearly total return of 8%, the cost of the loan is also 8%, which is quite expensive.

Some of the 401(k) plans have a special provision. Because of this, once you have borrowed money from the account, you cannot contribute additional funds until you have managed to repay the loan balance. Your plan might not specify this, but even then, it might not be possible to contribute as you are still repaying your loan.

Because you are unable to make additional funding, the money can no longer increase in value via compound earnings. Normally, your money, while invested, should double over eight years. The difference in the amount of money you could have earned will become greater if the missed contributions cause your employer to miss matches to the funds, as for you it represents free investment money.

The drawbacks of the 401(k)-loan discussed until now

have been since you are able to pay the loan back without facing any problems whatsoever. Most people borrowing from their 401(k) plans can pay them back in time, but in case you are unable to do so, the financial implications can be catastrophic. This is because defaulting on a 401(k) loan converts it to a withdrawal.

So, if you do not qualify for a hardship withdrawal, your remaining loan balance will be subject to taxation, at a minimum, at your rate of income tax. Also, if you are below the age of 59 and a half, you will incur a 10% early withdrawal fee on the borrowed amount.

Another downside of this type of loan is that if you lose your job or quit it, you will need to pay back the loan amount within a set amount of time. In 2018, some tax reforms were made and extended the time of repayment from 60 days after departure from your job to the next tax return date. This holds true only if the tax return date is a minimum of 60 days after leaving your job.

So, it becomes exceedingly difficult to leave your employer when you have taken out a 401(k) loan. Usually, you must pay back the amount in a period of five years, but here, you are forced to procure that money in less time. If you are not able to pay it back, the loan becomes a withdrawal, accompanying implications of penalties and income tax. So, taking out a loan you will struggle to repay could tie you down to a boring job and force you to make compromises by passing up better job opportunities.

Financial experts often advise against taking 401(k) loans because these assets may be your last option to survive a financial disaster. By accessing this option early, while other options are still available, you run the risk of depleting your 401(k), and when you are desperate for money, you would no longer have the financial cushion.

Borrowing from future savings is not a good financial

practice in general. This should be the time to examine what led you to this point. When you need to borrow money from your savings or life insurance policy, it means that you are living a more lavish life that you can afford. It is a red flag that tells you that it is time to make some changes to your lifestyle. This includes creating a budget and adjusting it, as well as coming up with a plan to clear all your debts.

Some people are highly confident in their abilities to pay the loan back within 5 years. But financial advisers warn that this hardly happens with a 401(k) loan. This is partially due to the large amounts of principal such loans have. On average, people borrow 11% of their 401(k) assets. Younger people in their 20s borrow much higher amounts equaling 26% of their savings.

Although the percentage of assets borrowed drops with increasing age, they offer little in terms of reassurance. This is because although older borrowers borrow less of their assets, they often have truly little time before retiring during which they have to replenish the funds.

Refinancing an asset with home equity or other kinds of equities is also a commonly seen self-funding technique. While there are a few advantages with this technique, borrowers need to be aware of the downsides as well. The primary one is of course that it costs a large sum of money. Often people take out a new mortgage in order to repay an old one, so you end up paying the closing cost, including the closing fees, application fees, title insurance, and origination fees.

Homes decline in value over time, and new lenders do not want to loan you more than what the property is worth, instead choosing to let the burden remain on your old lender. By refinancing, you end up paying 2-6 % of the borrowed amount, depending on your location. So, in order for it to be a worthwhile transaction, you need to save enough money.

But how can you tell if the amount of money you are saving through refinancing is enough? A clear indication of this is if you manage to recover the closing costs within a relatively short period of time. It might end up taking 7-10 years for you to recover the costs, if your new mortgage rate is 0.5% lower than the previous one. Depending on the closing costs you should target 1% savings at least for the refinancing to be worthwhile.

Refinancing your home into a new loan might not be a good idea if you have held a long mortgage term for several years. While your monthly payments might get lowered, you also keep extending the day you will finally own your home for good. And due to the laws of compound interest, even reducing the mortgage rate can end up in more long-term costs. So, in my opinion, it is better to choose a lower term corresponding to the time remaining on the original home loan. Lower mortgage rates come with short-term loans so while making the same monthly payments, you can take a few years off the loan.

You will see many mortgages lenders advertising zero-cost refinance, with no additional closing costs. But this does not come without a price, and in order to compensate, a lender might charge higher mortgage rates. If you do not have much cash on hand and are not willing to pay the closing cost yourself, refinancing with home equity may seem tempting, but the interest rate keeps accumulating over time.

If you plan to sell the refinance or home soon, then this kind of self-financing might prove to be advantageous for you. But for a period of 10-30 years, you will end up paying more in terms of interest than you would save in terms of closing costs.

Often when mortgage rates start to go down, borrowers sometimes chase after them, refinancing every time the rates go down by 0.25-0.5%. Because of this, they must pay closing costs each time that erodes their savings. So I feel it is wise to wait for the rates to fall by at least 1% or more before thinking about refinancing.

Home equity refinancing like a HELOC shares a disadvantage with the previously mentioned 401(k) loans, and that is the fact that getting so much easy money on your hands can make you spend more than you ought to. But if you know what you are doing with the money this option can be a blessing. It costs little to establish a home equity loan and the annual fees can go to a maximum of $100. Also, it is easy to access the money, and tax can be deducted from interest payments, like mortgage interest.

When you have so much money to spend at once, making big purchases does not hurt and furthermore, you get tax benefits from it. But if your financial situation turns worse, like in a case where your home loses equity (this happened to me) you will find that you do not have enough savings to pay the mortgage and the HELOC concurrently. In my case, I had to pick up another job and find extra income to cover the debt payments until I could pay my HELOC off fully.

Instead of the above-mentioned self-financing techniques, most people often choose to find people to invest in their ideas. This could include family and friends, angel investors, and venture capitalists. Approaching family and friends has its clear advantages, as you might get loans with little or no security unlike with banks and other financial institutions. You may be able to get a lower interest rate, or in some cases, no interest at all. The repayment method is usually longer, and they seldom ask for a detailed business plan from your end.

But you must understand that these can be complex transactions. They might damage relationships due to misunderstandings, as your friends will often offer you more than what they should, so they often demand repayment at a time which is inconvenient for you. Furthermore, they might want to increase their involvement in the business, which might not be suitable for you either.

Then comes the angel investments from wealthy individuals like business people, lawyers, and doctors. This can be one through the Chamber of Commerce or through word of mouth. Again, while this poses fewer risks than debt financing, you lose control over your business. The investor will chip in with suggestions on how to run your business and collect a large portion of the profits when you sell the business.

It is the same scenario with venture capitalist financing. These investors are aggressive and because they inject large amounts of cash into your business, they are highly likely to get involved in it. The more stake they have in your company, the more say they have in setting the direction. The venture capitalists can have as much as a 50% stake in your company, making you lose control over management.

If you are not careful, you might end up owning less than a 10% stake in your business, and most of the time, someone will buy this from you before the majority owners expand the business, so you lose millions of dollars worth of earnings. All the above-mentioned self-funding options are risky, and so you should consider other techniques that are sure to yield better results.

CHAPTER NINE: 2020 SELF FUNDING OPTIONS & BUSINESS STRATEGIES

"It is better if you can anticipate the need and get it early. This is because when your business is doing well, you will most probably get better terms."

A MAJORITY OF PEOPLE USE THEIR LINES OF CREDIT when they have some big expenses coming up or in an emergency where they need a larger amount of funds than they have in saved cash, like car-maintenance, or a home project. By using a line of credit, you can get the money you need whenever you want. You can borrow them from credit unions or banks, provided you are qualified. For a fixed period of time, you can only borrow up to a certain amount.

When you borrow money using lines of credit you only have to pay the interest. Upon receipt of interest, the lender will allow you to borrow the same amount again, this is called a revolving line of credit. Flexibility is the main feature here, you choose when to borrow the money, when to pay it back, and borrow the amount again, so long as you follow the terms and conditions. This includes always paying off the entire borrowed amount on time.

When the need for borrowing money arrives, there are roughly two options available to you- a line of credit, or a loan. When you take out a loan, a large amount of money is available to you and start the payment of the interest instantly; it doesn't matter when you are using the money. But with a line of credit, you get access to a fixed amount of money and you can draw it out as you need it. Until you borrow the money, you don't need to pay any interest.

Let's look at the personal line of credit first. These are bank loans resembling a credit card, because just like in a credit card, there is a specific amount of money that you can use whenever needed, for any purpose you like. A personal line of credit is not secured with an asset but your personal guarantee and to be eligible for one, your credit score needs to be 700 or above.

For some lines of credit, you need to pay an annual fee, and there is a limit on the amount of money you can borrow. After you have qualified, you can start drawing money for a certain amount of time from the bank account. This is known as the draw period, and it can last for many years. The bank either sends the money to the checking account or gives you special cards and checks that you can use, once you wish to start borrowing the money.

The interest starts to accumulate once you start borrowing the money, and you'll need to start with the minimum payments, at least. As you make the payments, your available line of credit will increase as these amounts will be added to it. Once the draw period is over, the repayment period begins, where you will have a certain period of time to pay back the remaining amount. If you decide to use only minimum payments the long term cost is going to be more.

The interest rates for personal lines of credit are much lower than credit cards, so many people prefer them to the latter. You also have more options when it comes to cash, unlike in a single-purpose, lump-sum loan. As long as the credit line is open, you can borrow incremental sums, repay the amount, and borrow it again. During this period, you need to pay interest on the amount borrowed, which is not the case for a regular loan, which you need to pay back in installments.

Although a personal line of credit bears certain similarities to payday loans, home equity lines of credit, personal loans, and credit cards, it has the unique qualities that make it a great option to borrow money when needed swiftly. Like a credit card, you can use it for any purpose, receive a statement every month that shows the expenses, minimum due payment, the amount owed, and interest charges. But the credit limit for a personal line of credit is usually higher, and the interest rate is lower.

Like a payday loan, a personal line of credit also involves a lender. But it is better than payday loans in the sense that you get to draw a much bigger amount lying between $3000 to $100,000, while for payday loans, you only get about $400. The interest rates for payday loans are extremely high (399%-521%), but for a personal line of credit, they are as low as 8% to 14%.

This line of credit can help you cover the expenses for a vacation, projects related to home modeling, your children's college fees, new furniture, medical bills, etc. So long as you don't exceed the credit amount, you can spend your money any way you like. However, like every type of credit, this too has its risks, and if you don't know how to handle it correctly, it could end up in a huge loss for you and put you in massive debt!

While applying for this credit line, you should remember that it is not secure, so you don't need to offer a collateral to the lender in case you default. However, as I said above most lenders require you to sign a personal guarantee. Meaning your personal assets may be at risk in the event of default. Some lines of credit like home equity are secured because your home's equity acts as security for them. Because of this risk factor, the interest rate for a personal line of credit will almost always be greater than a home equity line of credit.

So, you need to do some convincing on your part to ensure the lender that you are a decent credit risk. If you have a high credit score and have never defaulted on a single loan in years, it helps your case. You can also inform the lender about your income sources and how much money you have saved up so that they are convinced of your creditworthiness.

The amount of risk you pose depends on the size of your credit line. So you might want to consider limiting the requested amount of money to what you need to borrow, realistically. You should borrow the amount keeping in mind your ability to pay it back, as well as your income stream. For a lender, it is very important to assess your creditworthiness and do this by studying your history of repaying loans, your business risks, your income, and of course, your credit score.

Today, 25% of Americans use lines of credit to launch their businesses. This is mostly because of the advantages it offers over a regular loan. Unlike a loan, you can use the line of credit to make any purchase you want and you don't need to pay any interest for the amount you haven't used.

We mentioned the home equity line of credit before, and it is an option you can consider if you are looking for a more secure option. These lines of credit, also known as HELOCs, let you borrow money against your home equity while holding it as collateral. These lines of credit have changing interest rates, so with time, your payments may increase.

As a general rule, you can borrow an amount of money limited to 80 to 85% of the appraised value of your home, excluding the remaining balance on your mortgage. This interest rate set by the banks does not only depend on your credit score. Your income and credit history plays their respective parts as well.

Suppose the maximum amount is 75% of the appraised value and the value of your home is $200,000. So the amount you can borrow is $150,000. Suppose the price of the house was $160,000 and the value of the equity is $40,000, then you need to pay back $120,000 to the mortgage lender. The line of credit is then calculated as $150,000 minus $120,000, equaling $30,000.

If you don't own a house of your own or you don't want to use yours as collateral, you may choose to get a secured line of credit against your deposit certificate or your savings account. The negative aspect of this line of credit is, of course, the fact that if you are not able to pay it back, the asset will be seized by the lender to get their money back.

Let us now talk about the business line of credit. Also known as a revolving line of credit, these offer versatile loan options for small businesses. They help entrepreneurs keep pace with their recurring expenses and the seasonal fluctuations that are very common in businesses. A business line of credit generally provides a lifeline to about half of the business owners suffering from cash shortage.

As a business owner, you might think that you don't need more cash reserves as your business is already profiting. But whether your business has cash flow issues or not, you should keep aside a line of credit in case you need to expand or grow. Your short-term financial needs can be met through this low-cost line of credit.

Here, the lender allocates a maximum amount of capital to a business, based on the business credit rating and the current rate of cash flow. In this way, a business line of credit works like a credit card. In a conventional business loan, the business entity has to make monthly, weekly, or even daily payments in order to pay off the loan. But with a business line of credit, repayment occurs only when it draws money from the credit line.

Only when you take money from the credit line will interest be charged. The capital can then be used by the business whenever and however they want. Similar to a credit card, there is a fixed period to repay the loan, but there is no early payment penalty here, unlike a credit card. That being said, if you don't use your credit line, you may need to pay monthly maintenance fees.

A business line of credit can be unsecured or secured. For a secured business line of credit, there is certain collateral acting as a security deposit. One of the common collateral is property, but you can use other assets your business has, like inventory or equipment. Both borrowers and lenders prefer secured lines of credit. Since the risk is considerably less for a lender, they will normally set the maximum credit limit higher while offering lower interest rates.

If your business has a poor credit rating, you may only be able to take out secured lines of credit as it poses a much higher risk. Unsecured lines of credit do not involve collateral. Since the risk is high, the rate of interest is also high. Business organizations with decent credit reports and many years of experience can qualify for this line of credit at affordable interest rates.

If you should use a business line of credit, if your sales fluctuate seasonally, to give your business a much-needed boost during the low sales period. Maybe your clients make delayed payments and you don't receive it until about a month or so. In such a situation, you need funds to run your business, and a business line of credit is the perfect way to get that.

Suppose you manage to land a major client and you need

to increase your production to pay for the cost of materials. In that case, you can take the help of a business line of credit to cover the production cost. Sometimes, bills offer discounts if you pay them early, and if this discount is a large amount, you can consider paying it early by taking out a line of credit. This will help you save some money while your cash flow arrives.

For a business line of credit, the lender will try and determine your creditworthiness by assessing your annual revenue, credit score, time spent in business, and the strength of business credit and cash flow. You never know when you need to use a business line of credit, and for this purpose, you should start building business credit and set up a separate account for your business.

The lender will also consider the fact whether you can provide security for the line of credit. If you can offer collateral, a secured line will be much cheaper, and the lender will approve your request readily. As a good financing practice, you should not take out a line of credit when you are in dire need of it. It is better if you can anticipate the need and get it early. This is because when your business is doing well, you will most probably get better terms.

One thing you should keep in mind is that with most lines you only need to pay the interest for the amount borrowed. You can use the line of credit at any time, so you can get it early and use it during times of cash shortage.

Business lines of credit have some key differences with business credit cards. For the former, the credit limit is higher, and you can secure it using collateral. Also, when you draw from a business line of credit, cash is deposited into your bank account. Using a business credit card, you can draw cash, but you will need to pay a fee and the annual percentage rate is also higher. Business credit cards also often involve late-payment fees and annual fees.

For a small business that hasn't quite managed to establish its finances yet, business credit cards are suitable. But for mature businesses that need to pay for large expenses, it is better to use a business line of credit.

Small business owners have to manage a lot of things at once, initially. While managing the payroll, you might be picking up the trash or doing some cleaning. Small business cards can help finance daily expenses and can be hugely beneficial, provided you are using them responsibly. Also, through a small business credit card, you enjoy perks like purchase protection and rewards.

About 37% of Americans use small business credit cards for their businesses. The main determining factor for this credit card is your credit score. Using my 810 FICO score, I applied for and was approved for more than $100,000 of business and personal credit in 3 months, one lender approved me for more than $37,500 within 30 mins. As I am stressing, these funds can be used whenever needed. Now I don't need to borrow from a big lender or a bank to start my own projects and business deals. You need to make the best of the 0% interest-free introductory period every credit card offers initially. This means you have to pay zero interest on your credit card charge for up to 6 months or even a year.

You can use the line of credit provided by a small business credit to buy equipment and supplies. While starting a small business, you'll be naturally short on cash, and without credit cards, you might not be able to afford these. As a business owner, you know you sometimes need to spend money in order to earn it, but without a credit card, it can be quite difficult.

Your cash flow can be improved through a credit line as it gives you the ability to purchase items that allow you to finish your orders. Free-financing is an option available with many cards so that you can pay back the amount over time while incurring zero interest.

It can be a hectic process when you pay your employees using your personal card. You can manage the process smoothly by using business cards. This card can be used by employees for covering all expenses and every month you'll receive a bill containing details about your and your employees' spending. You can gain more control over your employee's spending as compared to when they use personal cards. You can freeze them as required and also decide the spending limits.

Often business cards have reward programs where you can earn points, miles, and cashback. Any purchase you make on your credit card can earn your profits, including purchases made by your employees. You can redeem the rewards through travel, merchandise, gift cards, and statement credits.

Like with personal credit cards, small business credit cards provide protection for purchase and travel. This usually includes collision waivers for auto rental damage, interruption insurance, trip cancellation, warranty protection, purchase protection, cell phone protection, and the absence of foreign transaction fees.

Small business credit cards also allow you to manage your account more efficiently. They provide year-end as well as quarterly summaries including the ability to use accounting programs to access the purchase records. Because of this, you can easily track your spending and simplify your financials during the tax season.

Yet another self-funding option to consider is Joint Venture. It is simply an arrangement between two business parties where they agree to combine their resources to complete a certain job or certain project. This can be any business activity or a new project. All of the participants in a joint venture are responsible for profits, losses, and expenses. This venture, however, is a separate entity and is independent of the business interests of the participants.

Although joint ventures are called partnerships, it is used loosely, and it can take the form of all legal structures. This includes partnerships, corporations, and limited liability companies, and other entities. Although it is more common to see JVs being formed for production and research purposes, they can serve a continuous purpose as well. Here, smaller and large companies can join hands to handle small and large deals and projects.

Let us talk about the advantages of joint ventures. With such a partnership, it is possible to utilize the combined resources of both companies in order to reach a common goal. While one company might have an efficient distribution network, the other one may boast of a sophisticated manufacturing process. Through a joint venture, both of these qualities can be utilized.

Through a joint venture, it is possible to lower the production cost of each unit. Sometimes a business might want to implement new advanced technology or which they need large sums of money. In that case, they can form a joint venture partnership with another business. The partners can also share labor and advertising costs.

The two parties in a joint venture each have their own areas of expertise, skill sets, and backgrounds. When these are joined by the means of a joint venture, both parties can benefit from each other's talent and expertise. All the partners' obligations and rights are mentioned in the document known as the JV agreement. This is done regardless of the legal structure of the joint venture.

This document clearly states the objectives, the daily operations, the initial contributions of both the partners, responsibility for losses, and rights to profits. This document must be drafted with care, otherwise, there might be a court settlement to deal with.

A joint venture also gives you an advantage in terms of territory. You can expand your market coverage by partnering with a company having a distributor network or a sales force. If you wish to take your export activities to other places, a joint venture can help with the expansion. When you enter a new market, you need proper documentation and licenses, and you also need to set up a local distribution network. But by entering a joint venture with a partner, you can take advantage of their customer base, contacts, and market knowledge.

JVs are commonly used by a company to enter a foreign market by forming partnerships with a local business. If a company wishes to expand its distribution network internationally, entering a JV agreement is a great way to do it. This way, they can supply their products to their partner, utilizing their efficient distribution network. Many countries place restrictions on foreign business entities, and for this reason, entering a joint venture with a local partner remains the only way foreigners can do business.

The IRS does not recognize joint ventures. So, how the two parties conduct their business decides how they pay their taxes. A joint venture pays taxes like any other corporation or business if it considers itself a separate entity. For example, if the JV operates as a limited liability company, then it will pay taxes as an LLC. In the joint venture agreement, they should be clear statements regarding how profits and losses will be taxed.

A joint venture is not a partnership in the strictest sense. A partnership is where two or more individuals form a business entity. In joint ventures, two or more entities join to form a new entity which is not necessarily partnership.

Before starting a joint venture, you must ask yourself

what to sell and how to reach the market you are targeting. Identify your competitors and ask them what it is that's allowing them to generate more revenues and reach more markets. Are there certain areas your business cannot access without partnering with a local business? Is there a business partner who can help you with horizontal and vertical market penetration?

You also need to consider how much human resources you have in operations, production, R&D, and marketing. Then you can see if there is a potential partner company whose resources complement yours. Joint ventures require combining resources, and you should be prepared to make sacrifices. It is wise to make sure you have access to the legal resources that will help you structure the joint venture.

Some businesses can bypass legal restrictions by partnering with local businesses. But you need to have access to a suitable partner who knows the local market like the palm of their hand. If you know about any joint ventures that are successful, you can reach out to them and learn from their experience. There is also the inevitability of reducing your workforce during the merging of two companies.

Entering a joint venture should not be a desperate last-ditch attempt to save your company. You should ask yourself if your company needs more credibility and support. It is a major project and one must consider all possibilities before jumping into it.

CHAPTER TEN: SETTING YOUR GOALS AND BREAKING FREE

"To get your organization up and running, it is important that you start the process of finding deals and then closing them as fast as possible."

SO YOU HAVE LEARNED ABOUT MINDSETS, LOANS, retirement plans, personal debt limits and credit. But what is your goal right now? I feel you should start by asking yourself, "what is my creditworthiness"? When it comes to applying for loans, the term that is often heard is creditworthiness. Now, the question about what this term actually means and its underlying importance is quite natural. It is vital that you understand the concept before applying for a loan.

Creditworthiness is the thing that lenders and creditors use to determine if you are deserving of new credit. This is the single most important thing that they look into before approving anything. Now, creditworthiness is determined by a variety of factors. Only after closely observing all these factors, do the lenders make a decision.

One of the several factors that the lenders look into is the credit report. In your credit report, information about how much debt you have, the present balance in every account, your credit limits, and the balances that are present. The report also cites instances such as due amounts, bankruptcies, and defaults.

Another criterion that is looked into is the credit score. Now, the credit score is usually represented by a set of three numbers, ranging from 300 to 850. The higher your credit score is, the more is your creditworthiness. This is an indication to the lenders that you are more likely to pay back in time. And the more creditworthiness you have, the easier it will be for you to get a loan along with a low-interest rate.

Apart from this, payment history also plays a major role. You are more likely to get a loan if you have made your payments on time when compared to someone who has a history of late payments and missed payments. The more financial stability you can portray, the more will be your overall creditworthiness. This is utterly essential because as much as 35% of payment history accounts for the credit score, which in turn is vital for your creditworthiness and approval of a loan.

For instance, in this example, Ashley has a 700 credit score along with high creditworthiness, and Brad has a credit score of 600 but with low creditworthiness. Here, Ashley will get a credit card with a limit of $5,000 and an interest rate of 11%, whereas Brad will receive a credit card with an interest rate of 23.9% and a limit of $1000. Due to the differences in credit score and creditworthiness, Brad has to pay more in interest than Ashley.

It is important to keep track of your creditworthiness, and if it is low, then you must take adequate steps to improve it. This is essential as, without high creditworthiness, it will be hard for you to get even a small loan, and when you do, the interests will be quite high.

The first thing that you can do is improve your payment history. You can do this by making timely payments. Do not delay or miss any payments. This will go a long way in building your creditworthiness. You can also set up repayment plans to a past debt that is due. Also, paying more than the minimum amount per month will not only help you to clear your debt faster but will also reduce the estimated late fees.

It is ideal to keep your credit card balances at 10% of the credit limit. But, realistically, this is always not possible but try to maintain the balances, at least 20% or less of the assigned credit limit. It is also important to calculate your Debt To Income (DTI) ratio and keep it at 28%, which is ideal. But, if that is not possible, then you must try to keep it at 35%.

If you are willing to make a sizable down payment on the loan you are applying for, then there are high chances for it to be approved even without high creditworthiness. Also, if you can arrange for a co-signer who has good creditworthiness, then the chances of your loan getting approved increases considerably.

To manage the cash flow or to overcome any gap in the finances of business, it is quite common to apply for a business line of credit. This is a kind of business loan that is much more flexible than an average business loan. By using the business line of credit, you only pay interest on the amount of money you have borrowed. You can repay it when you have enough money with the only stipulation that the borrowed money must not cross the credit limit assigned.

Applying for a business line of credit to fund your business is one of the most suitable financing options. I personally have used this option for every business I have and maintain. But, is it really easy to get it? The answer to this question depends on a variety of factors that differ from individual to individual. From the documents needed to qualify you, the kind of credit line you want, and the lender all play a factor into whether you get a business line of credit or not.

The documents that you have to submit are personal and business details of any existing debt schedule, business registration and license, contracts with other clients, information about, if any, stakeholders, information about your bank account, balance sheet, profit, and loss statements and business as well as personal tax returns.

To be qualified for a business line of credit, your business organization must be active for at least 6 months with annual revenue of a minimum amount of $25,000. You also must have a credit score of at least 600 or more to qualify, sometimes. In case of small lines of credit, these are enough. But, if you want larger lines of credit, collateral has to be displayed for obtaining it.

Before applying for a business line of credit, you must also be aware of the types that are prevalent. The two most common types are a short-term business line of credit and long-term business line of credit. Knowing in detail about the types available will aid you in making a sound decision.

These credit lines differ in the time period of repayment. In the short-term business line of credit, usually 6 to 12 months are offered as repayment terms. This is particularly useful for those who want to pay off their credit line relatively fast, and thereby, save a massive amount in the form of interest. However, in the case of a long-term business line of credit, the repayment terms extend to a time period, which is more than 12 months. These are ideal for those who are unable to make more payments and need more time to pay off the credit line.

After deciding on the type of business credit line you need, it is important to decide where to apply. Here also, you have several choices. You can either go to a bank, private funding institution and Credit Union. If you do an online search there are hundreds of brokers out there that have thousands of lending products you can review.

Banks are a more feasible option if you want to apply for long-term business lines of credit. The terms that they offer make this option extremely popular. However, there are several drawbacks. Firstly, you must have an exceptional credit card score. Secondly, you must have a business history of a minimum period of 2 years with annual revenue amounting to $250,000. Thirdly, it is extremely time-consuming. You most likely have to wait for a long time before your application is even viewed.

If you cannot afford to wait for a long time to obtain your business line of credit, then you may explore the option of online lenders. These are a more practical solution if you want to apply for a short-term business line of credit. The requirements needed by these online lenders are not as high or rigid as banks.

So, you do not have to worry too much about your credit scores or the display of detailed financial statements. They just need you to fill out the application form available and show proof you can pay the loan back. You can get back an answer within the next 2-3 days, which is quite fast. However, the interests charged are much higher than the banks. This is mainly because they obtain the funds from capital markets, which in itself is more costly.

There is also a third option for you to use and they are business lines of credit. You can apply for these lines at your local credit union. Now, these credit unions are either community-based or are occupation-based. To be able to apply for credit lines from credit unions, you have to become a member. In some cases, you can join the credit union by paying a small initiation amount and by using your account often. But, there is also a major obstacle. Credit unions usually do not have an online presence, or if they do, it isn't particularly strong. There are also very few branches and even fewer ATMs, which causes the drawing of money to be a real issue.

You must also know in detail about the other jargon related to business lines of credit like simple interest rate, annual percentage rate (APR), late fees, termination fees, payment processing fees, prepayment fees, and draw fees. If you are unable to understand this all on your own, it is always better to ask for a bit of professional financial advice before taking any vital step.

To get your business up and running, it is important that you start the process of finding deals and then closing them as fast as possible. When you close a deal quickly, you get the chance of getting your money back much earlier than it would have been if your deal was stretched out too long. Now, different deals required a different amount of time to be closed.

It is unwise to simply hurry and make some grave mistake, only because you want the deal closed as fast as possible. The most simple advice is to close the deal quickly but not in a hurry and only after going through the terms and conditions and profits numbers numerous times.

If you are making the deal and want it closed as fast as possible, then you can employ some ingenious methods. There are several sales strategies that you must become familiar with if you want to be consistent in closing deals faster.

The most common way to close a deal is to create urgency in the deal that you are offering. You can add a special offer which can be a benefit or a discount. It is vital that you convince the client or customer that closing the deal today would provide them with great benefits. It is normal for potential clients to seek benefits when closing a deal. For example – You can say, "We are offering an additional 25% discount just for today."

Another way to close a deal relatively fast is to engage in a conversation with the prospects that allows the closer to ask questions. After you have given the last pitch, it is important to end it with a question. For instance, ending it with "Is there any reason why you can't provide the raw material?" Now, depending on the answer to this question, you can proceed. If the answer is a no, then you have closed the deal effectively, but if the answer is yes, then you have another opportunity to address the problem. This way, you can interact with the prospects and know what issues they might have and then offer a solution accordingly. Nonetheless, it gets you to close the deal quite fast.

However, closing deals and arranging investors to fund your business is not an easy task. Oftentimes, these are not plausible notions. Also, borrowing a heavy amount of loans is a sure way to lose your business. Thus, it leads to a very simple question – is it possible to fund your own business? Well, if you have the financial intellect or are willing to heed to the advice of the professionals, it is very much possible.

Let's say, like me, you are venturing into or already are in the market of real estate. You can apply for a business line of credit or home equity credit line and use it to obtain a property. Now, you must make whatever repairs that are needed and then sell it at a profitable rate within the next 90 days to pay the line back and use it again. This is a strategy I am presently using. You can also put it out on rent. The rental income that you make will aid you to pay back the loan in time or give you time to refinance the money out to pay the line back. The time period is absolutely crucial. The sooner you sell the house or arrange a tenant, the more quickly will you be able to repay on your line. When you pay back your loan in time, you also increase your creditworthiness, and thereafter, your chances of getting another loan or line increase are much greater.

This is applicable for any business, but let's say you are dealing in the automobile market. You can use your credit line to buy a vehicle that needs some repairs. After you make the necessary repairs, you then sell the vehicle within 60 to 90 days at a profit. So you know, I shared this strategy with my cousin who is a licensed mechanic and is doing very well for himself. The time period for this type of venture is essential because first, it is a reasonable timeframe to fix what is needed. Secondly, it is enough time to sell the vehicle on an auto app for a profit turn around and do it again.

This 90-day strategy is something that will help you immensely if you can sell it with a high-profit margin. By utilizing this strategy, you can pay back the loan and save massive amounts. You can then use this money to fund your own business. But, this will not be favorable if you hold onto the asset without paying off the loan. In that case, the asset turns into a liability very quickly. This way, you do not have to be dependent on any angel investor for your business to take off.

FINAL WORDS

The main message of this book is that you should learn how to control your life and money better. Many Americans live in poverty today, and they don't know the first thing about banking and finance. So, they end up making bad purchases and are often forced into predatory payday loans that worsen their financial condition. This book encourages these individuals to pay attention to their credit score and rating, as this can be used to get much better deals on loans.

FICO 10 is being rolled out now, and people with bad credit scores will suffer because of this. So it is high time you paid attention to your credit score and take steps to improve it. This book encourages you to break out of the poverty mindset and take charge of your own life, making prudent investments and always paying back your payments on time so that you maintain a decent credit score. This will make you less of a credit risk, and lenders will be willing to lend you money at lower interest rates.

As you have read, most people belonging to the lower-income bracket do not understand the impact auto title loans and payday loans have on their wallets. These loans have very high-interest rates, and to pay them back, often you have to take another loan. Thus, your debt keeps on increasing, and you keep spending all your money to pay them back. As a result, you have no money to spend on essentials.

Moreover, if in the future as I mentioned, if you need to take out a loan from a bank, and they notice a payday loan in your credit history, they might not give you good deals, or even refuse to give you a loan outright. These payday loan centers are usually seen in financially vulnerable neighborhoods, where the people who take out these loans sink further into the pits of poverty, destroying their lives in the process.

This calls for a new financial approach. Credit rating is something that is not taught to kids in school, but it is the one thing that can lift you up from poverty. As you now know, banks and lenders judge your creditworthiness by studying your credit history, so you should always make your credit card payments in full and on time.

Today, many people are affected by the poverty mindset. An individual with this mindset thinks that money is hard to earn and all the environmental and societal factors are stopping them from living the life they want for themselves. This leads to a gradual acceptance of their financial condition, and while trying to make ends meet, they do not think about the future.

Then there is the blue-collar mindset where people don't want to give up the security their current job offers. This stops them from dreaming and exploring new things that will help improve their financial conditions. While the blue-collar mindset is somewhat necessary to keep the world functioning, it can be detrimental to the growth of an individual.

I believe that in order to improve your financial conditions, you need to be prepared to take educated risks, and that is what a blue-collar mentality prevents you from doing since you don't want to step out of your comfort zone. It is time you let go of this mentality and adopted the millionaire mindset instead.

A millionaire mindset involves carefully planning your finances, making good investments, and getting better returns. A millionaire doesn't necessarily live a lavish life with luxury houses and limited edition sports cars. As mentioned, they are often frugal and spend their money on things that are guaranteed to give good returns in the future.

This mindset involves planning for the next decade, when most people plan month to month. It involves creating multiple income streams so that the cash keeps flowing in and the wealth keeps on building. By making careful sacrifices and setting up plans, you can adapt to any changing market and overcome difficult financial situations.

This book urges you to understand your liabilities and assets. Learn what your strong points are and how you can put them to use. With so much technology available to us, we sometimes spend too much time these days on social media and Netflix, when that time can be put to better use. You can use that time to work on your business projects and convert your hobbies into something productive. Time is money, and by making good use of time, you can secure your financial future.

For a blue-collar worker to adopt a millionaire mindset, they must think of the future, while maintaining their work ethic. They need to learn that the times are changing, and bringing in new opportunities. Blue-collar workers need to grab these chances and realize that working smart is sometimes preferable to working hard. By having people working under them, and by building a team that helps them realize their vision, they can drastically improve their financial status.

It was my goal to educate you about several self-funding

options like personal and business lines of credit, small business credit cards, and joint venture deals. By taking advantage of these business and funding options, you can make some smart decisions and investments for the future. So you should start to set your goals now and realize your creditworthiness while taking steps to improve it. Also, start looking only for the deals you can afford and start funding them on your own to earn higher profits.

This book has identified the financial problems many Americans are having these days and have suggested some steps to rectify the same. By educating people about credit score and self-funding options, it has opened the door to a world of numerous possibilities. It urges people to take action to make their lives better and warns them about being complacent regarding their finances.

While this book covers a lot of topics, the one thing I'd like you the reader to take from this is no matter how bad your situation is, there is always something you can do to make things better for yourself and your loved ones. When you refuse to let negative thoughts cloud your mind and take action to improve your condition, you emerge as a true winner.

If you have enjoyed my book and the content was helpful please support this book by providing a review.

Get this additional Credit Boosting Guide 100% FREE!

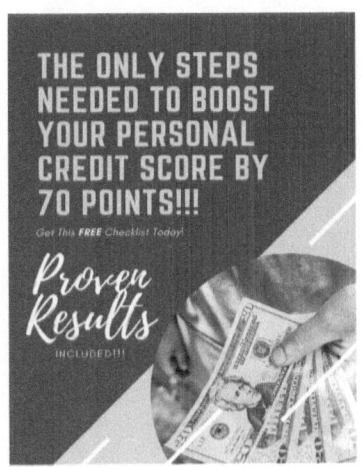

Many others are currently enjoying the benefits of insider access and the ability to get my books for FREE!

Yes, 100% FREE!

If you want insider access plus this Credit Boosting guide, all you have to do is click the QR code below to claim your offer!

ABOUT THE AUTHOR

G.E.S. Boley Jr. – He is a devoted full-time father, husband and Family Man who places Jesus above all else. George is a Martial Artist, Martial Arts Instructor with Multiple Black Belts in Taek-won-Do and Hapkido. George was a TaeKwon-Do National Sparring Champion and a Member of the 2007 USA Team. He is a Defensive Tactical Training Instructor, with training in hand to hand combat, stick and knife fighting and Freestyle Grappling. He is a health and fitness instructor and trainer, certified sports nutritionist, business entrepreneur, real estate investor, property manager, business consultant, and coach.

Along with training certifications, George has a Bachelor's Degree in Marketing and an MBA in Business. George has many life experiences and is passionate about learning and helping people in need.

REFERENCES

Bank of America. What is a Business Line of Credit & How Does it Work? Retrieved June 2020 Page url: https://www.bankofamerica.com/smallbusiness/business-financing/learn/understanding-business-lines-of-credit/

Center for Responsible Lending. Modern Day Usury: The Payday Loan Trap. Retrieved June 2020 at Page url: https://www.responsiblelending.org/sites/default/files/uploads/modern-day-usury-the-payday-loan-trap.pdf

Entrepreneur Inc. 5 Myths about Blue Collar Employees. Retrieved June 2020 at Page url: https://www.entrepreneur.com/article/337386

Entrepreneur Inc. 6 Ways to Develop a Millionaire Mindset. Retrieved June 2020 at Page url: https://www.entrepreneur.com/article/306652

Experian. What is a Credit Utilization Rate? Retrieved June

2020 at Page url: https://www.experian.com/blogs/ask-experian/credit-education/score-basics/credit-utilization-rate/

How Stuffs work. Assets and Liabilities. Retrieved June 2020 at Page url: https://money.howstuffworks.com/personal-finance/financial-planning/net-worth1.htm

Medium Inc. How to Defeat Poverty Mindset. Retrieved June 2020 at Page url: https://medium.com/@jerryfetta/how-to-defeat-poverty-mindset-9ec6cb6b5407

Medium Inc. The right mindset to have even as a blue-collar job worker. Retrieved June 2020 at Page url: https://medium.com/@achuyadavid/the-right-mindset-to-have-even-as-a-blue-collar-job-worker-3dd13e4aeb43

Medium Inc. Why Should I Build Capital with the Infinite Banking Concept? Retrieved June 2020 at Page url: https://medium.com/@ryandgriggs/why-should-i-build-capital-with-the-infinite-banking-concept-ffd5fdcb9fd8

The Balance. The Pros and Cons of Angel Investors. Retrieved June 2020 Page url: https://www.thebalancesmb.com/angel-investor-2947066